Endorsements

BORNE OUT OF A LIFE ....ment, persevering prayer, and passion for Jesus, here is a handbook packed with profound spiritual wisdom and filled with practical, down-to-earth lessons gleaned from faithful years in ministry. Everyone contemplating cross-cultural ministry and missions must read it and take it to heart. Yet its message is for anyone who is serious about following Christ. Written in a clear, engaging way, it will inform, challenge, inspire, and above all, drive you to your knees.

Stephen Seamands
Professsor of Christian Doctrine
Asbury Theological Seminary

CARISSA ALMA IS ONE OF MY HEROES. Her bold commitment and daring vision is reaping a great harvest for the Kingdom. This is one of the most thrilling stories of Christ alive today. You are cheating yourself if you don't read it.

Maxie Dunnam
President Emeritus
Asbury Theological Seminary

I HAVE KNOWN CARISSA for almost twenty years and have witnessed her sincere devotion to Christ, radical commitment to His mission, and unwavering faith for God's purposes to be fulfilled in this generation. Her work in Asia is a lesson to all who want to be inspired and instructed by a woman who has followed Christ in the sweet abundance of the crucified life.

Allen Hood
President of the International
House of Prayer University (IHOPU)
Associate Director of the International
House of Prayer in Kansas City

BURNED-OUT MISSIONARIES who return home sooner than expected, or those who stay longer than they should and grind out their ministry with little joy or fulfillment, often wonder "What went wrong? Did I miss God's call?" In this spell-binding book written from years of cross-cultural experience in Asia, Carissa Alma feeds those who are hungry to know the secrets to lasting the long haul with joy. Anchored in a deep spirituality with cross-cultural sensitivities the author handles many of the "hot potatoes" of mission, and provides a storehouse of sound advice for those launching a vocation of cross-cultural ministry. This will become "must reading" for all of our cross-cultural witnesses. Don't leave home without it.

Darrell Whiteman
Vice President, Mission Mobilization & Training
Resident Missiologist
The Mission Society

Thriving ~~SURVIVING~~
IN
CROSS
CULTURAL
MINISTRY

Carissa Alma

PAVILION BOOKS
PO Box 8653
Lexington, KY 40533

Visit our website at www.pavilionbooks.com

Printed in the United States of America
ISBN 978-0-9827-5192-3

Cover Design by Andy Coleman
Interior Design by Rhonda Dragomir

Dedication

To Tom Tanner

THANK YOU FOR EQUIPPING an entire generation of students to change the world! Thanks for pouring into me as a young clueless college kid. Thanks for giving me a push in the right direction. I would not be where I am today if not for your investment in my life. Most of all, thanks for being a true father in Christ to me over the years. I am eternally grateful.

Acknowledgments

I HAVE SECRETLY WANTED TO BE A WRITER for a long time now. Most people don't know this, but this is actually my second manuscript. My first one was about a caveman named George who invented the wheel (albeit a stone wheel). Unfortunately, no one else in his prehistoric neighborhood had invented the car yet, so he just walked around all day pushing the wheel from place to place. The book hit a climax when he bumped into a cave-woman, Susan, who was sitting perplexed on top of the wheel-less car she had just invented. Well, you can guess what happened next. They hit it off. They combined their ideas, and BOOM!— history was made.

I was in the second grade. I can still remember my feelings of pride at writing my name as both the author and the illustrator. I won the "young authors" award in my class. I was on top of the world! So, with that experience emboldening me, I am now endeavoring to write my second book: ~~Surviving~~ Thriving in Cross-Cultural Ministry. I have stirrings in my heart to write much more: about my life here with nearly fifty children, about the story of Joy Homes, lessons on parenting, stories of faith, children's books, and devotionals. We will see what God gives me the grace and time to do.

Many thanks to my beloved friends spread out around the world who have shared their struggles and joys with me over the years. Your insights and experiences helped me to form this book. It was written because of our conversations and prayers. Thanks to many other friends who helped me by listening to or reading parts of my book in its early stages. Since a lot of you are in sensitive areas, I won't mention names. Just know that many of you encouraged me along the way, and I am so grateful. For those of you who endured me reading portions of the book out loud, added to the conversation with your own stories and insight, helped me form a title and a pseudonym, and encouraged me along the way: thank you! (Rich S, Steve H, Tom, Melissa, Mark, Rekha S, Jasmine L, H Dej Anna, JG, Ames, Dylan F, Molly F, Kyle B, Ali B, TG, Prince F and many more!— THANK YOU!) And of course, special thanks to my Asian brothers and sisters who have walked with me, taught me, and have been patient with me over the years. I count you as my own family!

Special thanks to Darrell Whiteman of The Mission Society for his insight, guidance, and invaluable help as I began the book revision process. I am certain that his teaching during my seminary years helped deposit in me what I needed to last the long haul here in Asia, and his advice on the manuscript was much needed and appreciated. Thanks also to Steve Seamands for encouraging me to develop what began as a short ten-point article on my blog into a full-fledged book. His input into my life over the years has been a tremendous blessing.

My biggest thanks go to Kimberly Fleek, who painstakingly edited this book. I don't think she knew what she was getting into when she started! Thankfully, she stuck with it. Her own experience in East Asia was invaluable in the process of re-writing, and her edits and revisions helped craft my loose montage of thoughts into an actual book. I am deeply grateful for her offering her time and insight towards this project. Thanks also to Tommy Green of Pavilion Books for his wonderful help and patience in producing the final copy.

I also must thank all the missionaries who have paved the way before us. There are thousands upon thousands whose names we may never know, faithful workers of the Harvest who are beloved sons and daughters of God. They are a nameless, faceless generation of saints of whom the world is not worthy. I hope and pray that the insights in this small book will, together with God's Spirit, enable us to live out our callings with joy as they so faithfully did.

My ultimate thankfulness is offered to the One who has been so faithful to this child. I'm so in love with the One who loves me most! His steadfast kindness and leadership has been perfect in my life, and I seriously can't believe He is allowing me to fulfill the deepest desires of my heart through my life in Asia. I am especially grateful to Him for allowing me to experience His Presence through the process of writing this book.

Table of Contents

Foreword

HAVE YOU HEARD GOD'S CALL? Some may answer this question, "Yes. I know exactly where God wants me." Others will respond, "Yes, but I'm not sure where." Most may say, "Not yet, but I'm seeking." No matter which of these is your response, this book will speak to you. However, I ask one you to do one thing: don't just read it. Pray through each chapter.

Carissa gives a fascinating narrative about God's call on her life. You can sit back and enjoy the amazing stories of a young woman who has seen God at work, and that's a good read. You may want to read just to get wise advice about cross-cultural ministry and hear a captivating testimony, but you will be missing the more important thing this book offers.

Listen as you read. Carissa's story and words are forged in the fires of faith. Over and over again you will hear Jesus say, "Believe Me for this."

Your calling is an awesome privilege. Jesus invites you to merge your will with His! Out of that He designs a destiny that is beyond anything you could ever produce on your own. Unfortunately, though, too many believers misunderstand calling. They think that Jesus calls, and then it is largely up to them to make something happen.

If that's you, working hard to fulfill what you think God has called you to do, then you may think Carissa is fighting against your call. Believe me, she's not! Carissa believes in calling, but for her Jesus' call is not a command or a romantic notion to go into far-away outpost. It's a lifestyle.

I know this woman. She has given herself faithfully to a call for over thirteen years, and it hasn't been easy. Yet the Holy Spirit empowers her, the staff, and the children at Joy Homes. From scattered beginnings, Carissa now disciples a small band of radical believers. Their passionate love for Jesus will one day advance His Kingdom and liberate a population under the enemy's bondage.

She wants you to thrive in what God has for you. That means you can't go running off and try to make God's call happen in your own strength. Carissa warns to do so is certain defeat.

She's right. I too have seen the casualties of this kind of response. I remember several years ago sitting in the living room of a middle age couple who had given some years in cross-cultural ministry. Their calling had unfortunately spiraled downward into disappointment, offense, and even bitterness. They still loved Jesus, but their calling was now sitting on the shelf.

It doesn't have to turn out that way. If you want to do more than survive, then you must build faith and wisdom into your call. Carissa declares that God doesn't just fulfill our call: He is our call. That's why she continually invites you to worship, to wait, and to believe until God comes near.

If you are preparing for cross-cultural ministry, instill these values in your heart. Ask Jesus for the dynamics that Carissa shares. Listen to the counsel of an elder sister who has thrived in her calling. When you are on the field, open these pages and be reminded of what is really important. I believe if you do this, you too will thrive in ministry.

There's one more important thing. Some of you reading this book may have responded to God's call, but you feel it crashed and burned. Yes, mistakes do happen. The enemy may block us, or God even shifts direction. Carissa writes to you as well. God can redeem even the most difficult loss.

If you live in the pain of a lost calling, you're not alone. Paul himself, in his second missionary journey, was confused about what was going on with his calling. Here's the point, though: don't give up. Listen to Carissa's advice, and risk again for the breakthroughs of God's grace. Jesus creates a beautiful mosaic out of broken dreams and disappointments.

In essence, throughout the book Carissa shows you that cross-cultural ministry is a dance with God Himself. Remember: the key to a good dance is staying close to the lead Partner.

Mark Nysewander

MARK NYSEWANDER is a teaching pastor at Riverstone Church and Director of the Transformation Network in Kennesaw, Georgia. Mark has been a pastor, church planter and missionary. He is the author of three books.

Introduction

~

"You have made known to me the path of life; you will fill me with joy in your presence, with eternal pleasures at your right hand." Psalm 16:11

~

To UNDERSTAND THIS BOOK, you might need to know a little about me. About twelve and half years ago, I set out to Asia. I knew that I wanted to work with at-risk children in a third world country; beyond that, I had no specifics. I envisioned myself starting a drop-in center for children who lived on the streets in one of the larger urban centers of Asia. Instead, God led me to take in orphaned and abandoned children and to open a children's home. Thus began an incredible journey of living a radical life overseas.

I have since joined with a team of Asian friends, and we've adopted 48 beautiful children. We are raising them to know Jesus and to change the world! I often tell people that I can't imagine doing anything else: this is what I was made for. I wouldn't trade my life with anyone. I'm living the life of my dreams, even on a bad day (and trust me, I've had more than my share of those!)

Although this book was written mostly with missionaries in mind, I have a confession to make: I'm not sure I am one. I have always held this view in my heart. I love Jesus. I LOVE Him. I also love Asia, and I love children.

All three of these loves simply collide in Asia in the context of Joy Children's Home. I'm blessed and I know it! That being said, I think that most of this book would apply to any believer who has a heart for ministry and for seeing the dreams of God come true.

What follows has been born out of conversations I have had with friends over the past few years regarding missionary attrition (leaving the field), ministry discouragement, and burn-out. So whether you are already engaged in cross-cultural ministry, praying about going to serve, or simply have a heart for ministry, I hope that you will be encouraged by reading this book. There are quite a few of you reading who could actually add a lot more to this "conversation": I welcome your insight! I feel like I am only beginning to discover and to live out some of these truths.

There doesn't seem to be one definitive answer as to why missionaries return home earlier than expected. From my limited research, I see that many reasons are given. Conflict with other missionaries or with the sending agency, unrealistic expectations, loneliness, depression, financial problems, family problems/children's educational issues, burn-out, lack of community, lack of home support, and many more find their way onto the list. One common thread that seems to run between all of these, however, is that the missionaries almost always leave the field with a sense of discouragement and heartache.

I felt compelled to write such a handbook while watching friends and acquaintances struggle in trying to live out a missional lifestyle at home and abroad. I see their struggles and battles and their weariness, and my heart hurts for them. I write this because I wish someone would have written it thirteen years ago, sharing some of these insights with me from his or her own experiences. This little handbook isn't going to guarantee a happy, problem free life in cross-cultural ministry, but I truly believe these insights will help a cross-cultural worker to last the long haul— and to do so with joy. Yet as I said before, I am only beginning to discover and live out some of these insights, despite having lived in Asia for almost thirteen years.

This small book is not an exhaustive guide to a life of ministry or cross-cultural work. Really, it is more of a handbook that focuses on our hearts, our attitudes, and our postures as we prepare to engage in cross-cultural ministry. If we can grasp and live out these concepts, we will be used by God not only to effect change in the nations, but also to last a long time in ministry. What's more, we will have the time of our lives doing it!

You may find some details of stories missing, and I have also used first names only in many cases. These omissions, as well as the change of a few names and events and places, are necessary in order to protect many of us who are ministering in sensitive areas of the world.

I want to introduce you to a new style of writing. I call it "coffee shop style." You see, one of my top spiritual gifts is hanging out. I love to hang out with friends, and coffee shops are the ideal place to chill! This book is written with that in mind. As you read, imagine that we are just hanging out, talking about ministry, and talking about God's heart. (I'm even drinking a caramel macchiato as I type!))! So grab yourself a coffee, get comfortable, and start reading.

Chapter 1

Get Ready: Patiently Setting Yourself Before God for a Season of Preparation

The LORD is my light and my salvation— whom shall I fear? The LORD is the stronghold of my life— of whom shall I be afraid?

When evil men advance against me to devour my flesh, when my enemies and my foes attack me, they will stumble and fall.

Though an army besiege me, my heart will not fear; though war break out against me, even then will I be confident.

One thing I ask of the LORD, this is what I seek: that I may dwell in the house of the LORD all the days of my life, to gaze upon the beauty of the LORD and to seek him in his temple.

For in the day of trouble he will keep me safe in his dwelling; he will hide me in the shelter of his tabernacle and set me high upon a rock.

Then my head will be exalted above the enemies who surround me; at his tabernacle will I sacrifice with shouts of joy; I will sing and make music to the LORD.

Hear my voice when I call, O LORD; be merciful to me and answer me.

My heart says of you, "Seek his face!" Your face, LORD, I will seek.

Do not hide your face from me, do not turn your servant away in anger; you have been my helper. Do not reject me or forsake me, O God my Savior.

Though my father and mother forsake me, the LORD will receive me.

Teach me your way, O LORD; lead me in a straight path because of my oppressors.

Do not turn me over to the desire of my foes, for false witnesses rise up against me, breathing out violence.

I am still confident of this: I will see the goodness of the LORD in the land of the living.

Wait for the LORD; be strong and take heart and wait for the LORD.   PSALM 27

I WAS A COMPLETELY UNCHURCHED ATHEIST upon entering the University of Georgia in the early 90's, and then I met the Lord in a radical way towards the end of my sophomore year. My "call" to cross-cultural ministry came very soon after this, but it was very rough around the edges. I simply felt God pulling me towards a life in a developing country working with at-risk kids. So I went to my campus pastor, Tom, and I said to him: "I think

God wants me to go to some developing nation and work with at-risk children. Where do I sign up? Is it like the Peace Corps for Christians or something? Tell me where to sign up, I'm ready."

Tom took a few moments to explain to me the concept of a "missionary": I had never even heard that word! He explained that it wasn't quite like the Peace Corps, and he suggested some books for me to read. I was an avid reader, so I did. I read, and I dreamed about cross-cultural ministry. Later, during my senior year, I told Tom: "I'm going to the nations. I love Jesus. I'm about to graduate. I know I am called. I'm going within a couple of months."

Tom sat me down and said: "Carissa, you can go.... but it will be a short trip, because you just aren't ready." I was offended. "What?" I thought. "I love Jesus, and I know I'm called. I've been a Christian for over a year. What more do I need to know?"

When Tom suggested I go to a nearby seminary, I felt sick to my stomach. "Ugh!" I thought, "Another two or three years of studies? I am about to graduate college. No way!" I fought with God about it for several weeks; in the end, He won. So off I went, almost against my will, to seminary to study inter-cultural ministry. I am so *thankful* that I did. If I hadn't, I am certain that I would not be writing this book right now: I would be just another *casualty* of ministry. Am I trying to say that if you feel called towards cross-cultural ministry, you must go to seminary first? Not exactly.

What I *am* advocating is a season of being set apart, trained, and prepared for the trials of life in cross-cultural ministry, whether in seminary or elsewhere.

Love for Jesus and a call to join God's Mission simply aren't enough. There must be a season of preparation— a season of being set apart as you seek God for more of Him. The truth is that I could have gone into cross-cultural ministry as a new Christian right after college. I could have done it, and I may even have lasted a while on the sheer strength of my will. I might have even been used by God. Tom was right, though. It would have ultimately been a short trip because I just wasn't ready. For me, the practical teaching I received in my mission classes and the theological training of seminary set a solid foundation for me. The relationships I built during that time remain strong, and the inner healing and counseling I received during that season has been crucial to me in lasting the long haul here in Asia.

So what do I mean when I say get ready? I want to first address three key areas of preparation and then offer some practical advice.

Get Your Mind Ready

UNDERSTAND GOD'S HEART FOR THE WORLD. Understand God's Mission on the earth. Study the word of God to get it into your heart and mind. Get trained with practical solutions to real life cross-cultural issues and problems. Get some solid theology in your head and heart. Learn practical skills that will help you to live cross-culturally. There are so many others who have walked before you! Glean from their wisdom and advice, and learn from their mistakes. Set apart a season to be a learner, and soak in all that you can.

I had no context for true cross-cultural ministry in my limited experience: I was an absolutely unchurched, secular, humanistic atheist until I met the Lord as a college student. Although I had read the Bible a couple of times as a new Christian, I primarily knew only what others had told me. Seminary was crucial for me to gain head knowledge, heart knowledge, and a deeper understanding of the Bible, as well as church history and theology. My mission courses were exactly what I needed to help me make decisions as to what kind of missionary I would be, long before I ever entered cross-cultural ministry. I sat fascinated in courses that taught me to sort out just how much of my understanding of ministry was influenced by my own culture. I was challenged to believe God for signs and wonders, and I was challenged to a deeper life of prayer. All of these things helped me to become the woman of God that He wanted me to be long before reaching my host country.

I have a friend who felt called to Thailand from an early age, and she knew she would spend her life in Thailand ministering to women in the sex trade. She had passion and zeal and a desire to see God move in the nations, but unfortunately her season of training was only two weeks long. Her theology was so weak that when challenges came (which, by the way, they WILL), she crumbled. The suffering she saw in the lives of some of the young women she ministered to caused her to doubt all that she had heard from others. She folded. She actually started believing that it wasn't important if the women gave their lives to Christ— that helping them was "enough,"— and that by virtue of their exploitation and poverty they would be saved. I see this as a classic example of Matthew 4:16-17:

"Others, like seed sown on rocky places, hear the word and at once receive it with joy. But since they have no root, they last only a short time. When trouble or persecution comes because of the word, they quickly fall away."

Look at this time of training as a season of growing roots— roots that are going to give you the fortitude to last a long time in ministry. You seriously can't afford not to.

Get Your Heart Ready Spiritually

ONE OF THE MAIN REASONS I am advocating this training season is that many Christians carry offense in their hearts towards God. To be honest, I've seen way too much of this, and it frustrates me. When something bad happens, they blame God. When they encounter some disappointment or face an unmet expectation, they get offended with God. It's weird to me, but this kind of thinking is rampant. Why is that?

I am reminded of a young friend who traveled to Vietnam on a six-month internship with a popular missions group. After seven or eight weeks, when things became increasingly difficult, she began questioning God and His call. She had received confirmation in numerous ways that she was supposed to be there. Despite this, when struggles came, she became offended with God and returned home in week nine.

Contrast this with another story that took place a few years ago. A young family I know had moved to a difficult region of Sri Lanka to serve for a four-year term, working with local churches. Within three months of arriving, the husband was hospitalized with severe pain. After two days in the hospital, his symptoms improved, and the doctors assured his wife that he could go home the next day. So she went home with her two children and waited.

In the middle of the night, she received a phone call that would change their lives. "Your husband has died," the caller said. I can't even imagine the devastation she felt. She was alone, recently arrived in a difficult location, caring for two children, and the unimaginable had happened. Yet as she and the children got into a taxi to go to the hospital, she stopped and looked at them, weeping, and took their hands in hers to make a declaration: "God is GOOD, and HE is FOR us. We will trust in Him. We will not be offended."

This is exactly what I am talking about. There are saints in the world like this young mother, who was so solid in her knowledge of God that she could not be deterred by tragic circumstances. Yet we have a large population of people in ministry who get offended when things aren't as easy as they expected. I truly believe a season of theological training would help these individuals to gain a healthier understanding of God's ways.

First of all, they need to more clearly understand who God is and how God moves (theology). Shadrach, Meshach, and Abednego are great examples of those who had a great understanding of such theology. When they were threatened with being burned alive, they proclaimed:

"Even if we are thrown into the blazing furnace, the God we serve is able to save us from it, and He will rescue us from your hand, O king. But even if He does not, we want you to know, O king, that we will not serve your gods or worship the image of gold you have set up" (Daniel 3).

They had a healthy understanding of God's ways, and this helped them to walk with un-offendable hearts. Christians today likewise need to pray for hearts that will not fall apart when they hit a wall or encounter suffering or pain.

To get your heart ready, soak up scripture like a sponge. Learn how to cultivate a rich life in the secret place. Become a man or woman of prayer, and learn how to read and understand the Bible. Actively become three things: a Paul (teacher), a Barnabus (helper), and a Timothy (learner). Spend time teaching and mentoring and discipling others. Spend time with brothers and sisters who can encourage you while helping them in the process. Spend time as a learner, looking for a mentor to pour into your life.

When I looked for mentors, I found men and women of God who were older and more experienced than I, who simply shone by having been in the presence of Jesus. While many of my friends in seminary confessed they had a hard time spending time in the presence of Jesus (despite their devotion to Him), I am thankful that God established the importance of this time deeply in my heart. I sat at the feet of my mentors, and I asked a lot of questions. I listened, and I learned. God poured many life-long truths into my heart in this season at seminary.

Get Your Emotions Ready

BEING READY MENTALLY AND SPIRITUALLY is simply not enough. No matter what our background is, we all come into this walk with Jesus with some unwanted baggage. Use this season of preparation to be honest with yourself, and with others, about your struggles and weaknesses. Look honestly at your past and your own insecurities and shortcomings. Ask God to begin to heal you. Get counseling if necessary. Take some time with other believers to see what things you have believed that are false. Ask God to dispel the lies and speak truth over your heart.

I came from a terribly broken home, and I had been on my own since my teen years. Despite this, I went into seminary believing that if I loved Jesus and trusted Him, then everything would be fine. I had no idea all of the lies I believed about myself and about God because of my brokenness. God wants us to be wholly devoted to Him. How can we be wholly devoted to anything though, when we have hidden layers of darkness, pain, insecurities, bondage, and disappointment blocking that devotion? We must be honest about these things and get emotionally healthy before ever attempting to launch out into ministry. God is faithful to heal, to redeem, and to speak life into us, but we have to be open and willing to let the process of healing begin.

Don't ignore the deep things that God needs to deal with in your heart. It was in my season of preparation that God dealt with many of my wounds and healed my heart. Many Christians have repressed their deeper emotional issues, only later to find these things getting entrenched in bitterness in their hearts. Inevitably, the trials and struggles of life overseas cause these things to boil over and explode in unhealthy and ungodly ways. When you no longer have your traditional escape and defense mechanisms available, problems cannot easily be covered up or hidden. I've heard it said that missionaries are among the most broken Christians in the world. Brothers and sisters, let it not be so with you! Get your heart and emotions right. Spend time being honest about the dysfunction in your own lives. Get healing, and get freedom! There are Christian counselors available in many churches who can help you sort through things. There are also ministries whose main focus is to help you to process your emotions and walk through healing.

PRACTICALLY SPEAKING

Learn Something

I BELIEVE YOU MUST INTENTIONALLY set yourself before God for a season of training, and many mission agencies expect this as well. There are a lot of ways in which this can be done. For some, you may choose to attend traditional theological training in seminaries or Bible colleges that focus on cross-cultural ministry. For others, you may attend one of the incredible schools of ministry popping up around the world which offer solid biblical training and promote a rich life in Jesus. The International House of Prayer University in Kansas City, Missouri; Bethel School of Supernatural Ministry in Redding, California; Youth with A Mission Bases (all over the world); and MTI (Missionary Training Institute) in Colorado Springs, Colorado; are just a few examples. Some of you may choose to enroll in a *Perspectives on the World Christian Movement Course*, offered all over the United States in local churches. Many local churches are starting to see the need to prepare and train people in their church body in deeper ways and are offering classes and training programs to do so. However you choose to do it, you must learn to understand the implications of cross-cultural ministry and communication. Get trained! Even Paul, who was an expert in Jewish law, spent three years in Arabia and Damascus after his conversion. It was this season of consecration which prepared him for his radical life of ministry (Galatians 1).

Take a Trip

TAKE A SHORT-TERM VISION TRIP overseas to help discover the areas of need that best match your gifts and graces. Then, when you have a sense of what those might be, I *highly* recommend a short season spent in the place where you feel God calling you. It might only be a three to six month experience, but it should be long enough to give you a true idea of what you are committing to. I am not necessarily advocating this as a "trial period." Rather, let it be a season of living and exploration in which your eyes are wide open. Don't look at this season as a potential way out: look at it as the first step *into* a life of ministry. I remember when I first headed out to Asia, a friend said to me: "But Carissa, what if it's harder than you realize and you don't like it?" My reply to her was: "So what? What does that have to do with anything?" Take a short-term trip first as a learner; don't assume that just because it's not all you expected that you aren't supposed to be there longer term.

Find Your Niche

OBEDIENCE TO GOD'S CALLING to go is paramount. That calling, however, can take many different shapes and forms. As you seek to discern the "wheres" and the "hows" of your future in cross-cultural ministry, also be sensitive to your own giftings. Some of us are great pioneers, while others are great team players and gifted at supporting young works. Use discernment to find your niche.

I had good friends who felt called to ministry among the homeless in Johannesburg. They were gifted at support functions— helping an existing team or ongoing work. Because of situations beyond their control, however, they were thrust into a pioneering role and were expected to start a homeless shelter just months after their arrival. They left the area defeated and worn out after just eleven months. Another family was excited about reaching the lost in the Middle East. Because he was a gifted photographer, the husband was particularly excited about joining a ministry which created videos and media for ministries in that area of the world. However, when he and his young family reached their new home, they were shocked to realize that they weren't encouraged to develop relationships with local people. They left, completely discouraged, after two short years.

Both of these families could have flourished had they found their "niche," but instead they returned home early feeling disheartened and confused. As you pray into your future, think about your gifting and what kind of role suits you best. On a vision trip, go with your eyes and heart wide open, asking the Lord how you would best fit into that situation. Then make a commitment to that ministry, giving yourself to the work 100 %.

At the same time, remember to be realistic. No fit is perfect! Even in the best of ministries, you will find reasons to be discontent. You and your ministry partners are human, after all! Always keep a degree of flexibility so that, when day-to-day life is not just exactly as you pictured, you can guard your heart from offense and resentment.

**A Note to Newlyweds*

A LOT OF COUPLES WHO MEET and fall in love have a heart for missions and cross-cultural ministry. Because they feel a mutual calling and can't wait to start their lives together on this new adventure, many of them make the mistake of heading overseas during their first year of marriage. Larger mission organizations will not allow newlyweds to serve, but many smaller organizations do. I've seen it too many times: a young couple gets married and heads straight to 'X-city' within months. After all, they reason, they know they are both called overseas and don't want to waste time. In their minds, it just makes sense. With every fiber of my being, though, I want to shout at them: "NO—don't go yet! Marriage is hard enough without going to a cross-cultural setting and immersing yourself in full time ministry. Ministry will wait!" I've *never* seen it end well when a couple goes towards cross-cultural ministry too soon after marriage. Hear me clearly: I've never seen it go well. No matter how good your intentions are, no matter how gifted you are in ministry, no matter how deep your spiritual walk may be— do not go overseas in the first year of marriage. Period.

Consider these two examples and see which you think is better. Couple number one, Jake and Kara, get married and head overseas six months after marriage. Yet they come back during the third year of a five year term, angry, embittered, stressed, tired, worn out, and on the verge of divorce. Couple number two, Scott and Katie, chose to live as a married couple for eighteen months in the US before they head overseas. They are intentional about working through inevitable issues in their marriage, and then they venture into ministry in another country (one year later than Jake and Kara). Having had a safe place to build their marriage foundation, they complete their five-year term. They have thrived in ministry instead of just *surviving*.

These examples might seem a bit overly simplistic, but I've known couples who entered cross-cultural ministry early in their marriage. Many of them now feel completely disillusioned with the idea of ministry and a life overseas. Some are embittered towards the church. Still others are struggling with disappointment with God as well as a failed marriage. Take the time to go *well*— in a healthy way. You (and the community you join) will be glad you did!

**A Note to First Time Parents

FIRST TIME PARENTS OF INFANTS need to wait as well. It's a joy and a blessing, but first time parenting is also much harder than most of us expect. As a surrogate mom to nearly fifty children, I thought it would be a breeze when we got a newborn baby. I had no idea! Since most of our children were between the ages of three and seven when they entered our home, I had never before taken in an infant. I had heard mothers of newborns and infants talking about how exhausted they were, and I just didn't understand it. Now, after having raised my youngest, I admonish myself. I didn't have a clue! Relocating to a different country is hard enough for any of us. Add first-time parenting into the mix (of trying to adjust to a new culture) and you are just asking for unnecessary difficulties. Wait just a little while until that first baby is older. Even twelve months can make a big difference.

Listen to Your Leaders

IT IS TOTALLY IRRESPONSIBLE to send people into cross-cultural ministry without relevant training and emotional healing, and we need leaders who are unafraid to challenge those preparing to go. Personally, I'm so thankful to Tom that he "forced me" to get trained and to become whole! We need people like this in leadership who will lovingly confront other candidates and simply say 'NO' if they aren't ready. The candidates deserve that. At the time, they may be hurt, frustrated, or impatient, but in the long run it's for their good.

Pastors, spiritual leaders, and mission agencies need to confront emotional issues head on and to help candidates find healing and wholeness. I've seen too many people in ministry who have gaping emotional issues and huge wounds which have never been addressed. It may be messy to address these things, but we are actually helping them! Someone needs to ask the tough questions. Furthermore, you as a potential missionary need to go to some of these trusted leaders and ask them, "Am I ready? Do you see any issues in my life that need addressing?" If you are scared to ask someone, you probably aren't ready!

I've had people come to join us for a season in ministry who later had to leave earlier than expected because of difficulties. Then I heard people say after the fact: "Oh, yeah, I had a couple of red flags concerning that person." I want to shout at them: "Why didn't you say anything? Not for our sake, but for theirs!" Those going should have the fullest blessings of both their sending agencies and their home church. There are way too many missionary casualties in cross-cultural ministry otherwise.

Be Patient

GOD OFTEN GIVES US a sense of *urgency*, but God is never in a hurry. I've seen both younger and older people struggle with the idea of 'waiting' once they feel called. The younger ones seem to feel they are "wasting time" if they do not go immediately upon being called: they get passion and wisdom confused. Many of these young people don't want to take the time to persevere through a season of training, and I often think to myself: "How are you going to persevere through hardship and suffering in ****** when you can't even persevere through four years of college in America?" I hear some of them saying: "God's told me to go, so I'm going! I'm ready! The people there are lost and dying and I have the good news!" I seriously have to bite my tongue sometimes so that I won't say what I'm thinking: "Don't kid yourself. The world doesn't need you that badly. You know Jesus and you love Him, but as you are right now you really don't have a lot to offer. If you go now, you will maybe even do more damage than good." Older individuals, on the other hand, sometimes assume that their life experience makes missions training unnecessary. To them I ask: "What does life experience in America have to do with solid training for a life overseas?" You must be patient.

THE FIRST SECRET TO LASTING the long haul in cross-cultural ministry is to patiently set yourself before God for a season of training. Don't miss out on this crucial preparation season for your life in global ministry! You seriously can't afford *not* to do this. There will always be a sense of urgency when it comes to the Kingdom of God, but God is never in a hurry. Be strong, and take heart. Wait for the Lord. Wait for His perfect timing.

Chapter 2

Be Filled:
Cultivating a Life of Prayer

*"I have come that they may have life, and have it to the
full." John 10:10*

THERE ARE MANY REASONS cited for missionary attrition.
One major reason I have discovered personally— after
having watched friends return home early, broken, worn
out, burnt out, embittered, and disillusioned— is that
they are lacking a supernatural life in the Holy Spirit.
I've seen too many missionaries return home, unsure if
God loves them or cares for them, or even unsure that
He exists! They seem so defeated and discouraged, convinced that there is no such thing as "life to the fullest."

I will never forget a simple teaching I heard as a student that impacted me in a life-changing way. The speaker taught about being filled with the Holy Spirit; He talked about the power of prayer and fasting and the power of a life *lived* in the Spirit. As He spoke, I literally felt a flame in my heart being fanned. That teaching did something to me, and a life of prayer was birthed that day in me in a unique way. I've definitely struggled and failed along the way, but a lifestyle of prayer became a part of my DNA from that point forward. I'm so grateful to God for instilling this truth into the core of my identity from early on.

When I gave my life to Jesus, I had an amazing heart change. Then, within a few months, someone explained to me about a deeper life in Jesus in the Spirit, and I saw examples of this kind of life displayed in some of my friends. They didn't worry what others would think, and they had a sense of tangible joy. They had peace and assurance and contentment that I had no idea how to walk in. They talked with Jesus as though he were a real man— close to them, intimate and warm. I wanted this life, too.

I asked some of these friends to pray for me. As they laid hands on me and prayed, I began crying out to God with every fiber of my being. Something shifted in my heart, and I was totally filled with the living presence of Jesus. It was suddenly easier to hear God's voice, easier to listen, easier to say YES to God, and easier to choose Him. All at once, I seemed to know the depth of God's love and passion for me, and this fueled my heart for Him. Nothing was the same. I was undone. The best way for me to characterize being filled with the Holy Spirit is reaching a new level of total and absolute surrender. You can call it whatever you want to— baptism of the Holy Spirit, being filled with the Holy Spirit, absolute abandonment to Jesus, total surrender— but I am convinced that we MUST experience this supernatural encounter with Jesus if we are going to last for the long haul.

Be filled. You must be filled with the Holy Spirit! There is no way you can make it in cross-cultural ministry without having experienced the depths of Jesus through the Holy Spirit. I'm not talking about being saved; I'm talking about being filled. There is a deeper abundant life, and it is available to all who would simply ask. You have to be empowered supernaturally by the Holy Spirit. If you aren't, the enemy is going to eat you for lunch. You must be filled. You cannot get away with a mediocre life in the Spirit in cross-cultural ministry.

Let God have every single part of your heart. Hold nothing back. Recognize that you are dead without Him. Be filled with the Holy Spirit: it will be a defining moment for you as a believer. Then be filled daily, and seek God diligently. Pray at all times. Don't just have prayer as a part of your life, but live a life of prayer!

I can remember sitting under the teaching of an older woman who was known for her deep prayer life. She would say: "Listen closely, I'm going to teach you the secret of prayer." We would lean in, straining lest we miss the secret of having a rich prayer life. Then she would say: "Pray, pray, pray." That's the secret. Sounds too simple, huh? Shouldn't it be a deeper and more mysterious secret? No! It's simple. Pray! You want to learn to be a man or woman of prayer? Then start praying.

Be filled. There is no other way. You can't do any of this in your own strength! Be filled. Learn to lean into Jesus. Learn to discern His heart for you. Learn to hear His voice. If you don't learn this deeper level of a life of prayer, the enemy will have his way in your life and you will not last a long time in ministry— period. You must learn to enjoy God and enjoy God's presence. I can't imagine trying to last twelve years in Asia without the supernatural presence of the Holy Spirit in my life. I would have died— in more ways than one.

A college team visited the homes for a short-term trip a few years ago, and I had watched as they spent time praying together as a team each morning. They struggled with weak, pathetic prayers for about fifteen minutes, and then they were done. As I began to share with them some of the miraculous events surrounding our home and ministry and explained the difference it makes when you seek to live a life empowered by the Holy Spirit, their mouths fell open in disbelief. This team was made up of Christians, but they instantly recognized that something was missing. They looked at me incredulously, and asked: "How can we have this? We believe you. We see it for ourselves in this ministry.....how can we be filled? What do we need to do?" I explained more to them, then I called Jonathan and Amy— staff members and good friends— to pray with me. We laid hands on them and prayed for them as they cried out for God to change them from the inside out.

Every single one of the team members had a supernatural encounter with God that night. In their own words, they were "flooded" by the Holy Spirit— but it didn't stop there! Their morning prayer sessions had previously been marked by sleepiness, weakness, and apathy. The next day, though, they prayed for five *hours* straight! They were filled with joy and delight and simply glowing when they came out of prayer. They thought something must be wrong with the clock because praying for five hours had felt like 45 minutes to them.

One of their team members, meaning well, cautioned them that they were on a spiritual high and full of zeal because they were on a mission trip. She said that the Christian life is marked by highs and lows and that they shouldn't expect their lives to stay like this permanently. I tried to hold my tongue, but I just couldn't. "No", I disagreed, "that's just not true. If this were just a high, I wouldn't have made it here this long. This is the way we were *meant* to live. It's not a phase! It's life on the edge with Jesus. There is no other way."

The team traveled for several more weeks around Asia, and they came back with amazing stories of divine encounters along the way. Then I recently met up with two of the guys on the team (who had come four or five years ago). They told me that of the seven students, six are already involved in or headed for full time ministry. They are still going strong! They have also shared about this deeper life with so many others, and as a result many, many lives have been affected.

When I contemplate the lessons on prayer that God has taught us in Joy Homes, I can point back to several key principles. One of these main lessons has to do with perseverance in prayer, and I can honestly say that God has been building this into the very fabric of our hearts.

I'm reminded of Jacob in Genesis 32:22-31. He wrestled with God. He contended with God. He refused to let go of God until He received the blessing he was seeking.

People often stand amazed at the miracles we have experienced in Joy Homes and the crazy breakthroughs we've seen. They don't seem to realize that we have seen many of these breakthroughs come after a season of persevering prayer. Similarly, as I've counseled younger American Christians throughout the last ten years, I find that many of them have absolutely no framework for this kind of persevering prayer. They only pray about something once or twice, maybe even three times, but then they impatiently become offended with God when they don't receive any kind of breakthrough. It seems like "wrestling with God" is a lost art altogether. America's fast food drive-thru culture doesn't really lend itself to the idea of having to press in and wait on the Lord.

Here's an example. People usually marvel when they hear the story of how God gave us a bus, but it's easy for them to gloss over the real story. We tore out a picture of a bus from a magazine, and we taped it to our wall. Then every single night for months, we prayed as a large family.

"Father, we ask you to give us a bus," the kids prayed in their broken English, night after night, after night, after night, after night. "Jesus, You can only do this miracle. You can only give us a bus."

We never talked to others about the need or made the need known. Then, after *months* of praying without ceasing, a man in the US emailed me and said something like: "Carissa, been praying for you. Do you need a bus?" He got together with our church, and they gave us a brand new bus. It's one of a thousand great stories of God's faithfulness to our little band of believers and our precious children, but let's not forget the lesson. PERSEVERANCE IN PRAYER!

I'm reminded of another story of persevering in prayer. Samyan, one of my boys, disappeared a few years ago. He was eleven years old at the time. He had come to our home on a series of trains after "running away from home" at seven years old. He was a great kid. He did well in school, had a good heart, was a great athlete, and was an all-around well-adjusted kid. His biggest downfall seemed to be his complete absent-mindedness, and we adored him.

One Tuesday night, Samyan had gone to lock the gates, but he didn't return. There was a huge festival in our nearby village, and we suspected that he might have gone to see it— the lights, music, dancing, drinking, etc. Yet, choosing from all of the boys who we thought would actually run away, Samyan would have been our last pick. He was content, happy, and seemed to be super secure. We thought he might have been kidnapped at the festival, as a lot of the people there were drunk and a little on the wild side. There had also been a lot of cases in our city of kidnapping and crime in general, and we were frantic.

We began searching for him. We divided up into teams, searching nearby villages, moving towards the city center, and combing the entire area. There was a team of four policemen at the festival, and we asked them for help. They just looked at us and said: "Don't worry...you will find him." They said that we would have to wait a day and file a report at the station, and then after that they may be able to help. They refused to do anything.

Samyan went missing at eight p.m. It was extremely cold for our area at the time, and we all had on jackets, sweaters, and shawls. Samyan had been dressed in shorts and a thin t-shirt— no shoes, no jacket, nothing else for cover. We were worried sick about him. We searched the festival grounds, the villages, and the city until midnight. Those that were too small to help with the search (the girls and the boys under nine years of age) sat in the home and prayed their hearts out. Finally we all came together again and realized that there was no way our efforts were going to find Samyan. We had searched in the pitch black night and had not found a single clue as to what had happened to him. Before we sent them to bed, we prayed again with the older boys. Through tears, Anuman prayed that even though *"Samyan might be walking through the valley of the shadow of death ...he would fear no evil, for God was with him."* Many of the adults in the home then gathered in my room, and we began praying, pressing into God for a breakthrough.

To understand the situation, you must know that there is no centralized system here to deal with missing children. Between the many different languages spoken, the sub-cultures, the poverty, the lack of education and the corruption, there is very little recourse at all when it comes to missing children. The return rate for lost kids is extremely low, and unfortunately even those who are supposed to help often don't. In some cases, the children are thankfully rescued or found. In the majority of cases, though, there is no final answer. Missing children just seldom return. Our only hope for Samyan to return was Jesus!

Anyways...back to the story. We were praying and crying and worshipping, asking God for a miracle. We felt as though we should pray for Samyan's immediate return to our home, even before the sun came up. So we did not pray vaguely: "Lord, please bring him home soon," but rather: "You *must* bring him home tonight!" As a staff, we were sure that God wanted us to pray without ceasing, to persevere, and to contend with Him for Samyan's safe return. So we prayed. We pressed in and asked God for a miracle. Faith rose up in our hearts and we prayed without ceasing for several hours. Faith arose to almost "demand" that God do what He promised and to hear and answer our prayers— cries of: "God....YOU MUST BRING HIM HOME BEFORE THE SUN RISES!!!!"

Some of the staff were exhausted and went to bed around 2:30 or 3:00. Jonathan, Amy, and I stayed awake a little longer, praying, talking, crying, and then beginning to doze off around 3:30. We would wake up every few minutes, look around, pray, and listen. Then at 4:30 AM, Amy and I both shot up straight and looked at each other. "Something happened!" we both said. We ran outside and looked over the wall and there he was. Dressed in his shorts and t-shirt, shivering on swollen legs, was Samyan! We brought him inside, hugged his neck, put a blanket around him, and just hugged some more. He cried and seemed to be in mild shock.

It turns out that he had run away after all— kind of. He had been playing outside instead of locking the gate, and he didn't want to come inside. So he ran off playing for a while. When he turned around later, he realized he was lost. There are no landmarks, main roads, or even streetlights leading to our home, as it is surrounded by two villages interspersed with the forest. Samyan told us that he had started crying and searching for the way home, but it was dark and cold and he had become completely disoriented. He walked and walked and walked, searching for the way home, but he was completely turned around. He ended up about ten miles away from us!

Finally, about one in the morning, he saw something he recognized and turned that way. He jumped over a compound wall of someone's house, trying to get home. A policeman stopped him at that point, and Samyan told the officer that he was lost. The policeman said: "You are on the grounds of a jail. Do you want to go to jail? Get out of here and go home." Scared, Samyan took off running and eventually found his way back home. He was chased several times by packs of wild dogs along the way, one of which chased him all the way to our neighborhood! He said he kept praying, and God gave him one verse which strengthened him and helped him to find his way home. What was that verse? *"Even though I walk through the valley of the shadow of death, I will fear no evil...for you are with me!"*

Samyan made it back home— chased by dogs, weary, ashamed, tired, sore, cold, thirsty, and hungry, but he made it home. It was right before the sun came up, and it was a major miracle. I can't express to you how big this was for us. With all the reports of missing children who are forced into child labor, harvested for body parts, kidnapped for ransom, abused, exploited, etc, it was impossible for us to trust in man for Samyan's return. We had needed God's direct intervention, and God was faithful. We are still on cloud nine about Samyan's return!!!

God wants to move mightily in our lives and through our ministries, and a lifestyle of prayer and reliance on the Holy Spirit is one amazing way to experience this kind of reality. Perseverance is often the first key. We have learned a second principle of prayer, though, that is also important to grasp as you begin to wrestle with God. As you contend with God, you will need to hold your heart carefully. There will very likely be times of disappointment and unanswered prayer.

We've seen numerous miracles over the years, but we've also seen some disappointments. The most obvious one to date is the loss of one of our younger children, Kanita. At the age of four, she was brought to us by a social worker. Three words described her: precocious, fun-loving, and light-hearted. Kanita was a JOY! The social worker brought her to us after the death of her grandfather, the only relative known to be living. Then suddenly, four years later, her 'presumed dead' mother showed up. She said that she had suffered atrocities at the hands of her husbands' relatives, but she had been searching for her stolen child for over three years. The police arrived with a court order to take the child back immediately.

Kanita had never known her mother, and she was terrified. They took her by force within an hour of her mother's arrival. It was a gut-wrenching experience from every angle. We prayed and prayed for her return, or we prayed that at least that she would be allowed to be with us for a few weeks to help her transition in a healthier way. Our prayers went unanswered, and we haven't been allowed any contact since. It is heartbreaking.

Remember the concept of not being offended with God? In the midst of this huge heartbreak, we were solid enough in our understanding of God's character to proclaim: "God is good. He is for us. This situation is painful, but we chose not to let our hearts become offended." There will be times when we contend with God, and we may not receive that for which we believe. We will, though, come out of it touched and changed by God in the process.

One final important principle of prayer is that it's impossible to speak of prayer without speaking of fasting. John Wesley said: "The man who never fasts is no more on the way to heaven than the man who never prays." I wish I could write this from a position of having mastered this spiritual discipline. Even though we at Joy Homes are like spiritual kindergartners in the life of fasting prayer, we clearly recognize that something is unleashed through fasting. We've seen time and time again God breakthrough into our lives after a time given to fasting and prayer.

Early on in our life in Joy Homes, I felt God lead us toward a lifestyle of weekly fasting. On one of the first of these all-day fasts, we were praying for breakthrough in the area of provision. I'll never forget it. Around five pm, the kids were really dragging. They could barely walk or move, and some of them were almost to the point of tears, complaining about cramps. I said to them: "Why don't you go drink a big glass of water?" They looked at me with surprise and asked, "You mean we can have

Carissa Alma ||

water when we fast?" My poor children thought that fasting meant going without food AND water, even when it was 100 degrees outside! Once they recovered from that fiasco, the kids began to love it and have frequently asked for more. "Carissama, can we do a three day fast soon?" they ask. Ha ha.

In one of our early experiences, we felt led to fast and pray for three nights for a breakthrough for two of our boys— eleven year old Jao and his nine year old brother Jaidee. They were in danger. Their parents had died under violent conditions, and they had been placed in a government facility at the young ages of seven and five. A social worker had tried for several years to find them a permanent home until we took both of them in early 1999. They blossomed in our home, growing healthy physically, emotionally, and spiritually. Then, out of nowhere, the social worker who handled their case called us and said that a long-lost, poverty-stricken uncle suddenly wanted custody of both boys. It turned out that he— their deceased father's brother— wanted both boys to work his land. He knew they were old enough at nine and eleven to work the farm, and they would not be allowed to go to school. They would essentially be slave-laborers. Of course we immediately fought and said: "No way, these guys are thriving here! They are happy, healthy, and have great futures ahead of them!" We fought, but the fight was short lived. No one would help us. With the very little child-advocacy in Asia in general, we had no legal recourses. Heart broken, I even contemplated taking both boys and hiding somewhere. Our entire ministry and home would have been shut down if we refused to return the boys to their uncle,

31

though, and another twenty-five children would have been out on the streets.

We were all heartbroken. On Wednesday, we were told to have the boys ready by the following Sunday. We knew that it was time to press into God for a miracle. So on Thursday, we started a three day fast— a few of the staff, eight of our oldest children (ages seven through eleven), and me. We asked the Lord to intervene and to fight for our boys. We prayed our hearts out!!

On the third night (Saturday) of our fast, Jao just stopped. He said: "We can go eat dinner. My uncle just changed his mind. He's not coming to get us."

I just looked at him and waited, thinking to myself, "The poor little guy is hungry."

Then he said: "I saw a drop of Jesus' blood fall from the sky way down to earth and it fell right on my uncle's head and he just changed his mind and said we could stay." So, we let eleven year old Jao lead us in a prayer of thanks, and we went down to the kitchen and ate dinner. Ha ha!

The next morning, we got a phone call from the social worker. She told us: "It seems as though the uncle has changed his mind and he said that he would not bother you again. He cancelled his train tickets. The boys are yours for life." Can you imagine the joy in our home that morning? No words even come close to describing it! God began showing us through this that prayer and fasting go hand in hand, and the practice of fasting has been part of our home ever since. Jao is our oldest— almost twenty-one years old— and is in his third year of college. He starts seminary next month, where he is preparing to return to his villages to do community development and plant churches among unreached people!

Remember please: as you set out for cross-cultural ministry, you *must* be filled with the Holy Spirit. Don't make the mistake of thinking that you will develop a richer prayer life once you begin your ministry: how your prayer life is now is most likely how your prayer life will continue to be. If you are too busy or too unmotivated to pray now, what makes you believe it will somehow be easier to do once you reach your destination? Develop a life of prayer and fasting *now*. Learn how to wrestle and contend with God for victory. Understand the glorious riches of a life sold out to Jesus! Beloved friends, you won't last long without a supernatural life in the Spirit!

Chapter
3

Fight Well: Understanding the Truth about Spiritual Warfare

"Finally, be strong in the Lord and in His mighty power. Put on the full armor of God so that you can take your stand against the devil's schemes. For our struggle is not against flesh and blood, but against the rulers, against the authorities, against the powers of this dark world and against the spiritual forces of evil in the heavenly realms. Therefore put on the full armor of God, so that when the day of evil comes, you may be able to stand your ground, and after you have done everything, to stand. Stand firm then, with the belt of truth buckled around your waist, with the breastplate of righteousness in place, and with your feet fitted with the readiness that comes from the gospel of peace. In addition to all this, take up the shield of faith, with which you can extinguish all the flaming arrows of the evil one. Take the helmet of salvation

and the sword of the Spirit, which is the word of God. And pray in the Spirit on all occasions with all kinds of prayers and requests. With this in mind, be alert and always keep on praying for all the saints." Eph. 6:10-18

I WANT TO TELL YOU STRAIGHT UP. For those of you heading out to the nations, you are about to enter a war zone. You will encounter spiritual darkness and powers you've never seen or experienced before. Certainly, you have nothing to fear if you are abiding in Christ. For the sake of the people with whom you minister, though, don't underestimate the powers and principalities of this present darkness. Our battle is not against flesh and blood. You *will* have power encounters with powers of darkness. What will you do? What will your response be? Will you believe God for supernatural miracles or will you pretend this physical world is all there is? You have to be grounded in the reality of the spiritual war raging around you. f you don't know anything about spiritual warfare now, please endeavor to learn now— before you head out!

At the same time, don't go overboard and over-spiritualize every hardship as an attack from the enemy. I have friends who literally see a demon behind every tree. Every single time something goes wrong, they proclaim that the enemy is working against them. One day, I was with some of these friends while they were working in an internet café. I had the habit of saving my work via thumb drive. They didn't. So, when the electricity went out suddenly (as it frequently does), they started muttering: "The enemy is working against us. He is threatened by us." I started laughing, and I held up my thumb drive and said: "Or, maybe God just wants you to go buy a thumb drive."

Another frequent mistake made by many missionaries is that they blame anything they don't understand on powers of darkness. As missionaries, we definitely need discernment. As an example, consider some of the many festivals in Asia. During one such festival, I witnessed a parade of men and boys, dressed in yellow, beating drums and chanting. These men and boys all had spears pierced through their bodies, faces, backs, and cheeks; they were bleeding and disfigured by the spears. They were obviously in a drug induced mental fog as they marched to show their undying dedication to their deity. I think it's safe to say that there was a level of darkness and oppression over that parade and festival.

In contrast, there was another festival where everyone involved had dressed up in green. They also chanted and beat drums as they marched through the streets, this time carrying banana leaves and singing. Their cows and bulls were all decorated to the hilt. A visitor who was watching this with me stated: "Wow, this country is so dark." I started laughing as I replied: "This is the harvest festival. It has no religious connotation, but is celebrated by Hindus, Muslims, and Christians alike." Use discernment. Just because it's different and you don't understand it doesn't mean that it's dark or evil.

In some parts of Asia, families have a habit of decorating the outside of their homes with something called rangoli. I see it often outside the homes of Christians, Hindus, and Muslims. The best way to describe it is artwork outlined in white powder, with different color powders filling in the lines. Some rangoli design is simple, while other designs are breathtakingly beautiful. It's traditional cultural artwork— nothing more. I have actually walked with missionaries who kicked the rangoli as they walked in to a house or muttered under their breath: "the blood of Jesus, the blood of Jesus," as they walked past it. I wanted to laugh out loud. That's like kicking an American child's sidewalk chalk art and proclaiming the blood of Jesus over it as you walk. What? Don't assume that it's dark and evil just because it's different.

Use discernment! The same missionaries that kick over the rangoli sometimes fail to recognize the very real attacks of the enemy that cause discord and disunity in their marriage and family. Determine to pray daily for your marriage, your family, and your hearts. Don't let things remain hidden in the dark where they can gain power. Understand the big picture. Pray for discernment. You seriously won't make it long without it!

That warning being given, there will be real situations that demand deep responses. Let me give you a few examples from my time in Asia. During my earliest time there, I volunteered in an orphanage. I was there for several months, full time, living on the campus. The care in the home was substandard, and the spiritual atmosphere was dull. So I began praying for miracles, for more of Jesus, and for a breakthrough for these kids to encounter the Living God.

As I walked through the dorm, where more than fifty kids slept on three tier bunk beds, I prayed for them. I stopped over each child's bed and just blessed them and prayed for them as they slept. When I came to one six year old little boy's bed, I paused. This boy had never opened his mouth and had never talked, but he could make sounds. He was what the textbooks would call "an elective mute." His mother had tried to commit suicide with him when he was a baby, holding him in her arms as she jumped in front of a train. Hat-ai, the little boy, was thrown aside by the force of the train, and this orphanage took him in. During the next six years, Hat-ai had not spoken one word.

So as I stood over Hat-ai's bed, I prayed for him. "God if there is something that is keeping him from talking, then just show me." It wasn't the most powerful prayer ever prayed. I was just praying in a general way. Well, I almost wet my pants when he started convulsing in his bed immediately and shaking uncontrollably. I scooped him up, woke up a fourteen year old girl who had just met Christ the day before, and asked her to translate for me and to pray with me for Hat-ai. She joined me, and we carried him downstairs to my room. We prayed for him for all of fifteen minutes. We commanded the enemy to loosen his grip over Hat-ai. We asked God to heal his heart. We prayed for his heart, for his mind, and for every part of him. I was clueless, having had very little experience in these types of things. Within a few minutes, though, little Hat-ai started speaking fluently in his mother tongue. We started crying. It was unbelievable! He told us in his broken mother tongue: "Thank you, I'm so happy! That demon was holding my tongue so tightly."

This was a first for me. I had little framework or experience for this, but that's what happened! I woke up some of the older kids in the orphanage to share about this miracle, and several of them gave their lives to Jesus. A lot of other amazing things happened in this season; within three months, almost all sixty-five kids in this home gave their lives to Jesus!

That was one of many power encounters that I had in my early days in ministry, and we saw incredible fruit that had long lasting ramifications. For example, there was a young ten year old boy whom the authorities had written off as insane. Initially, he looked and acted like the children in the government insane asylum. He would beat his head against the wall, rip off his clothes, and throw feces at us if we got near him. We fought for him in prayer and fasting for a period of several weeks. Finally, we not only saw him gain total freedom, but he also gave his life to Jesus as his memory was restored. We were able to return him in his right mind to his parents who had been searching for him for *six months*.

I have, in several instances, come face to face with the demonic. Spiritual warfare is real, and real powers of darkness do exist. From time to time God has enabled me to see what it is that is actually happening in the heavenly realms. I am convinced that if He took the scales off of our eyes so we could see what is happening in the spiritual realm at all times, we would be undone. However, you won't make it long in ministry without a keen understanding of the reality of spiritual warfare taught in Ephesians 6. My life in Asia has been marked by this reality. At Joy Homes, we have seen supernatural miracles, but many have come after intense seasons of spiritual warfare.

There was one very dark time that God used to awaken me again to the reality of the war in which we are living.

I had been on a trip to a neighboring country, and I was getting ready to return to the children's home. When I called the home from the airport to let them know what time I would be arriving, one of the staff said to me: "Carissa, Mae-noi's mother came here and filed a police case against us and wants her daughter back." My heart sank. No! Not MAE-NOI!

Honestly, no matter what child that news was about, my heart would have had the same response. "No, not Kenye", "No, not Areva", etc. I love these children! This news seemed to hurt more intensely, though, because Mae-noi was just three years old. She was the youngest and most vulnerable in our home; she was our baby. I sat on the plane and just cried and uttered some pathetically weak prayers.

Mae-noi's father had died of AIDS, and her mother was sick with AIDS. A social worker had brought Mae-noi to Joy Homes when her mother was entering a hospice care center, so the whole situation seemed shady. The reasons her sick mother now wanted her back were not clear. There was apparently some kind of land dispute, and she needed to prove to her late husband's relations that Mae-noi was still alive in order to get some of this land. It was a complicated situation to be sure. What made it worse was knowing that here, where there is very little actual child-advocacy, the parental rights almost always outweigh the rights of a child.

For a three year old child (a girl no less) from an AIDS-affected family to soon be left parentless in one of the poorest areas of our region made her fate extremely precarious. We knew without a doubt that if Mae-noi went with her mother, that we would never see her again. Her life would almost certainly be filled with injustice and suffering; this is simply the reality we face here. Her mother even told us several times that she would have no choice but to sell Mae-noi after getting the land.

So I stepped off of the plane into this huge crisis. The involved police tried to talk Mae-noi's mother out of taking her, but in the end they supported her wishes. Mae-noi cried; she didn't want to go. Although she recognized her mother (she had only been with us one year), she wasn't happy to go. She cried and cried and cried, and with everything in me, I wanted to fight. I wanted to fight physically, legally, or however else possible to keep Mae-noi with us! However, as her mother stood in front of us, I clearly heard God say: "I want you to fight for her Carissa, but not in those ways. I want you to fight in prayer! Teach the children to fight, lead the staff to fight, and fight for her. Bless her mother, but fight for Mae-noi." I felt a huge weight hit me, and brokenness overtook my heart. I recognized it as the hand of God.

So, we all said goodbye to Mae-noi, and I cried like a baby. It was overwhelming. She was so sweet and small and vulnerable, and I was sure we would never see her again. I held onto a strong sense of dread, expecting her life to be "doomed." Only a very faint sense of hope mixed in somewhere with my despairing thoughts. During that time, I wrote to several good friends and asked them to join us in prayer. I wrote: "My heart is just broken, and I feel so discouraged by this loss. I have hope and even a sense that God will do this...bring Mae-noi back.....but still am struggling with this particularly hard hit. Does that make sense? Please pray for us here. I know that I am gonna sound like a big whining baby when I write what I am about to write, but I will write it anyway..... I just feel like my entire life has been about 'fighting' for everything.....as a non-Christian.....as a Christian.....I just feel like not much comes easy and I have to fight for everything.....I am a little tired of fighting and probably feeling a little self-pity.....ha."

My friend wrote back these words: "I don't interpret your words as selfish. Don't be too hard on yourself. You have just taken a hard hit. I see more that you are battle weary. Yes, your life has been one of battle. Yet your life has also seen advancements in the Kingdom that go beyond most people I know. It still doesn't take the sting out of what is going on, but I want to encourage you that you are out-flanking the enemy in so many areas. I'm convinced the only weapon he has against your little group is intimidation. He found a way to slip into the gate and hurt you in a big way. We will stand with you in the battle. I wish there was some other way to define life as we wait on the Lord besides war, but that is what it is and you are on the front line. Just be sensitive to the time you need to get some rest and encouragement. We love you and we love the way you battle. You are not selfish— just weary of the war. I know the Lord will bring retribution against your adversary over what has happened. We stand with you."

As I read these words, I just started crying. I mean, I was really, really weeping. Suddenly, it was like the spiritual veil was lifted again for a moment, and I saw it: I saw the *reality* of the huge spiritual war that we are in. It's real. If we are going after God with our full hearts, we are going to engage the enemy— period. It's a war.

Why do I keep forgetting that and looking around bewildered as if something strange were happening to me? (1 Peter 4:12-13) Why do we all keep forgetting? The words in my friend's email which hit me the most clearly were: *"I wish there was some other way to define life as we wait on the Lord besides war."*

That was a revelation. There is no other way to describe what is happening around us. The Kingdom of Heaven is breaking forth on earth, but there is resistance and a price to pay in scars and blood and pain. This is war. The Kingdom of God is advancing. I am not being melodramatic: I am being realistic. Do we believe that the Bible is just a metaphor, filled with some nice ideas from which we can pick and choose when the mood strikes us? Or is it real? I am convinced that we are in a major war, not against flesh and blood, but against the unseen powers of darkness. Why do we keep forgetting that?

So I felt God leading us to fight, to pray, to believe, to beg, to knock, to rejoice, and to thank Him! I also felt that God had a tremendous thing to teach us all through this about "contending in prayer" for real, tangible, seemingly impossible victories. This lesson was not only for me, but for our whole home— and for our kids especially. Our nine and ten year olds needed to know what it means to *pray,* to *fight,* to *press in* to God for victory. What better way for God to teach us this than by allowing our youngest and weakest family member to be taken from us? Everyone was attached to her— the boys, the girls, the adults, and friends of our home. She was our baby!

So we got the kids together and prayed. We prayed our hearts out, again, and again, and again, and again, over the coming days. The Sunday night after Mae-noi was taken, we spent much of our fasting prayer time fighting for her. It was an amazing time of prayer and worship, and God gave at least eight or nine of us specific words or visions about Mae-noi's return. One of our boys, Jao, shared a vision where God said to Him: "Before Carissama's birthday, she will hold Mae-noi again. She will see her walking down the road with her own two eyes."

For all of us that night, God gave a strong sense of assurance that Mae-noi would come home. My heart shifted, and the heaviness that I had been under— the hopelessness I had felt— was completely taken from me. I felt free, and I was 100% certain that she would be returned to us (not in a "we will see her somehow, somewhere, in the future, or in heaven" kind of way, but as in we would see her return to Joy Homes soon!) We thanked God and rejoiced.

Okay, to make a long story short, Mae-noi's mother changed her mind. She had encountered roadblock after roadblock in her village, and she said she felt "something like darkness" trying to push against her. She told us that a huge cloud had chased her all the way back to our city (a 12 hour bus ride away), and she felt "compelled" to bring Mae-noi back to our home! They arrived after two weeks of being gone. True to Jao's vision, it was February 28— one day before my birthday! We rejoiced together and thanked God. Mae-noi's presence in our home is a like a constant, tangible, visual reminder of God's victorious power and immeasurable grace.

I found myself incredibly thankful for this lesson. I know it had a good ending, and that makes it easy to be thankful. I would like to think, however, that I would still be just as thankful if we were still praying for Maenoi's return. I don't know that I would, but I do know that God taught our home a life-long lesson through the ordeal. Our kids' prayer lives were already pretty strong, but this crisis just took us deeper in God. It has been an incredible blessing to us. I know that there are parts of God's heart that are impossible to access outside of this kind of spiritual conflict— this kind of battle and warfare. So I am sincerely thankful for God's kindness and graciousness to me— to *us*— in teaching us this lesson. He has given us a reminder of what life is really about as we wait on Him.

It is impossible to thrive in cross-cultural ministry unless you learn to live in the reality of spiritual warfare that is taught in Ephesians 6. You must recognize that this world is *not* all there is, but that there are spiritual things happening behind the scenes all the time. You must be prepared to recognize the enemy's tactics and schemes, but also to know that you weren't created to keep taking blow after blow. You were *created* to *stand strong* and *fight*. Learn this lesson, and learn to fight well. The battle, and the victory, belongs to our God.

Chapter 4

Live Simply and Trust Wildly: Learning to Simplify as You Take Leaps of Faith

"And my God will meet all your needs according to his glorious riches in Christ Jesus." Phil 4:19

I KNOW MANY PEOPLE who felt called in high school or college to a life in overseas mission. Some even had amazingly specific calls. Over the years, though, somehow life (most often financial issues), "just got in the way" of their call. Decisions were made, and things "just happened." Ten years later, their original calling seems to have faded away. I'm not trying to criticize: many of those friends are living amazing lives for Christ in the daily grind of

American life. What I *am* doing is giving a word of warning to those seriously praying about embarking on the journey.

Make every decision count. Don't "just let" things happen! Pray about every purchase you make, every lifestyle decision you make, and every single major choice you are given. Think about it! Does it lead you closer to your goal of engaging in cross-cultural ministry?

Some of my friends had school debt and had to work to repay it. Instead of choosing a simple lifestyle, however, they actually began accruing more debt. Others who felt called towards cross-cultural ministry allowed the lifestyle of their peers to influence them and soon were living way outside of their means. Money is a very touchy subject for many people, but Jesus talked about it more than He did any other topic. I've seen it happen too often that people actually convince each other (and themselves) that certain unnecessary things are necessary— even at the expense of Biblical truth. We are masters at deceiving ourselves that we must have more! This crazy love of money and material things is one of the biggest stumbling blocks to a life of a radical abandonment to Jesus and cross-cultural ministry.

Take, for example, a couple in their late twenties. As college students, they knew beyond a doubt that God was pulling them towards a certain country in South Africa. They got married after their junior year of school, dreaming of South Africa. They went to mission conferences, and they even began to explore the mission-sending process. Because they had some school debt, they decided to both work to pay off the debt in preparation for a life overseas. This was a good choice.

Within one year, however, this couple was convinced that buying a house was a good investment. After all, why throw your money away on rent when it could go towards equity? At least that is what well-meaning Christian friends advised them to do. Within two years, unforeseen problems arose with the house, and they sank further into debt. The couple managed to work through much of that debt, but then they incurred more financial obligations: a new car, new furniture for the house, a new HDTV, and the newest gadgets. Within another year, while they had the insurance from their jobs, they decided to start a family.

You get the picture, right? Seven years after graduation, they have worked off a lot of debt. Yet they have also incurred many new financial obligations, actually increasing their debt, and put their plans for cross-cultural ministry on hold for a longer season. They have become slaves to their lifestyle, feeling trapped and unable to do anything but to maintain the status quo. Chances are, unfortunately, that this "hold" will become a permanent thing. I've talked to many couples in their forties and fifties who say to me: "I wanted to be a missionary, but it never worked out." This sounds better than: "I made a series of bad choices that kept it from happening." Again, I'm not trying to judge people's lifestyles or decisions. For those of you on the verge of making some huge life decisions, though, I *am* advocating caution and intentionality. Simplify your life for the sake of the gospel so that you can release funds for the Kingdom of God. Train yourself to be satisfied and content with little. This will also allow you to better identify with 90% of the entire rest of the world.

As we talk about finances and living simply, it's impossible for us not to talk about radical faith and trust. God loves to be trusted! He loves it! God is searching for people who will radically believe Him for the impossible. Countless times, God has provided in miraculous ways for me personally, and He has also provided for our children's home and ministry. We've been led by God not to solicit funds or make our needs known, but rather to pray and ask God for every need. It's not a conviction I think that everyone should share, but it's a personal lifestyle choice that I feel God has asked us to make. We feel God's presence as we wait for Him, and we sense God's joy. From land to buildings, tables and benches to a playground, bunk-beds to firecrackers to food, God has showed up in some miraculous ways over the years!

For me personally, seeing God's provision started for me as a new Christian at the University. I had just read the Philippians chapter about God supplying all of my needs, and I didn't know any better than not to believe it. I just took God at His word, and I began praying for a job. "God, I need a job that is around my school and student teaching hours, only requires a few hours, but pays a lot of money," I said. *While I was praying*, the phone rang. My friend at the other end said: "Carissa, I was just thinking about you. Do you need a job, one where you only have to work a few hours but get paid a lot of money?"

"Wow!" I thought, "Life with Jesus is AWESOME!" That simple answered prayer was the beginning of a life of radical trust for me. I found anonymous money gifts tacked up to bulletin boards at our campus ministry, and I found money on the ground. Strangers handed me money, and a random check for $165 came the day rent (which was $165) was due. When I headed to seminary and my needs were even greater, God continued to provide in radical ways. I got a lucrative babysitting job the weekend before rent was due. Someone handed me fifty dollars in cash on the day my gas tank was empty. Someone sent me an unexplained check for $78.15, and I received it the day my alternator broke (and happened to cost $78.15 to repair). Each month, when expensive seminary fees were due, I found checks, anonymous cash, gifts, and anonymous deposits which would cover the fees to the exact penny. I have a thousand more examples from that season, but that's another book entirely.

I have even found unexplainable errors in the banking system that left me with money. When I tried to clear them up, I was told there was no mistake. For example, just a few years ago, I bought a round trip airline ticket to the US for $1,500. I charged it on my credit card, got the ticket, flew to US, and waited for it to show up on my credit card. It never did. I called the credit card company to ask about it, and they said they could do nothing until the airlines reported the charge. So, I called the airlines and told them that the charge hadn't yet come through. They pulled it up and informed me that the credit card company had already paid for the ticket and there was no problem! Who does that happen to?

As I took steps towards Asia, I continued to see the radical supernatural provision of God at work (again, that's another whole book). At Joy Homes, we have watched in awe as God provides for every single one of our needs. We've not done any PR or any self-promotion, and we have not built any websites. We just pray. We trust. We wait. We receive. It sounds too simple to be true, doesn't it? It's not. We've seen God's hand provide for us through the body of Christ over and over again, sometimes in the craziest and most creative ways.

I am reminded of our very first Christmas together in Asia. With twenty children living at the home, God had been teaching us about child-like faith. What better way was there to teach me more about this than through the children themselves? On Christmas Eve morning, the kids asked me and the staff for firecrackers for Christmas day (a local tradition is to shoot off fireworks during major religious festivals). We just told them to pray and ask God to bring us some firecrackers, so pray they did. Big-time!

Twenty little ones, ages three through ten years old, gathered around in a circle to pray. They were so cute as they pleaded with God in broken English: "Jesus you can only bring us the crackers." "It is your birthday, you can only do this nice miracle for us." "Don't you want to celebrate your birthday big?" "You are the good Father, you are always giving us nice things. You can only do this." They prayed for about ten minutes.

Around three o'clock that day, a beat up, dirty old box came in the mail. As I started to open it, the kids were going wild. "Carissama, it's the firecrackers we prayed for!" I shook my head and laughed, telling them I didn't think so. The kids insisted. "Yes, it is!" I looked at the oldest, ten year old Jao, and said, "Honey, it's not. It's illegal to send firecrackers through the mail." He laughed at me and said, "You are just kidding. It is definitely the crackers we prayed for. Oh Carissama, always you are teasing us."

52

Well, I continued opening the package with the kids gathered around me, and what do you know? It was *full* of firecrackers! What's up with that? An old beat up box full of firecrackers!? It was loaded down with M80's, flashbombs, dynamite, 1,000 firecrackers, sparklers, and tons of heavy-duty fireworks. ao just looked at me and laughed. "Carissama," he said, "you only told us to pray and that Jesus would give." His expression said to me: "Why in the world are you surprised, when you told us that Jesus comes when we call?" I laughed and then lied: "Yeah, I knew it all along that HE would provide. I was just kidding....." WOW! It was the faith of a child.

Please don't misunderstand: this is not just another cute story about my kids. I am convinced that the secret to the Kingdom of God is that simple. When we, His children, call to Him, He comes. What's so unbelievable about that? Does God's blessing stop among "orphans?" Is it only for them to witness miracles of love and provision? Or is it for us too?

Jesus loves us. He keeps His promises, and He loves to come when we call to Him. What are you calling out to Him for today? What are you believing Him for today? Have the faith of a child. We are just kids, and He is our Father. He is waiting, wanting, and longing to show Himself to those who will ask and believe.

I think it is impossible to hold any kind of discussion on supernatural provision and simplicity without mentioning radical giving and the ability to live unattached to money and materialism. As I look back on the times in my life where I radically received a gift from the Lord, I notice that they were often tied to times where I had been challenged to give radically. I remember, for example, at least a dozen times while I was at seminary when I felt moved by the Lord to give away my last twenty or thirty dollars. Every time that I did this willingly, it was pure joy! I loved waiting on God and seeing how He would come through for me as I threw myself on His grace.

One day, I walked into the seminary bookstore to buy my books. I had been challenged to give my last thirty dollars to missions on that Sunday morning, but I had wrestled with God about it a bit. After all, the semester had already started, and I hadn't yet bought one book! I had one dollar to my name, and I spent it at the food bank buying cereal and bread. I was absolutely broke, and I still desperately wanted milk for my cereal! Still, I prayed as I walked into the bookstore that Monday morning, recently reminded of a book by Norman Grubb about Rees Howell and his radical faith. I thought to myself, "If I believed that God is who He says He is, then I would get all of my books— all two hundred and fifty dollars' worth— and I would just get in line to pay for it, even without money." So I did just that. I got in the line, and I waited for a miracle of provision. However, my faith still wasn't quite as strong as Mr. Howell's, and I kept getting in and out of the line! Despite this, God honored my heart. An hour later, after a series of events that are hard to explain, I walked out of the bookstore with *all* of my books *and* twenty dollars in cash!

There have been other times where I didn't give with joy, but rather in reluctant obedience. Despite my heart's condition, though, God has still come through for me. One Sunday at church, we were challenged to give to-wards a certain cause/overseas mission. As I opened my purse to pull out five dollars (out of the forty dollars I had to my name), I remember thinking: "I'm practically broke, but I'll give a little." Suddenly, I felt challenged by God to give it all. I fought and fought with God, then finally decided that I would compromise and give *twenty* dollars. (For the record, "compromising" isn't the best tactic with Jesus). I gave the twenty dollars, but throughout the rest of the service, I felt sick to my stomach. I could not rationalize giving away my last twenty dollars, but I knew I was being disobedient. Finally, the Holy Spirit got the better of me, and I went up after the service and gave away my last twenty. As I got into my car and got ready to pull out of the parking lot, an older man in our church knocked on my window. He smiled and said that the Lord had spoken to Him during the service that he was supposed to give me two hundred dollars. He handed me a check, and I started crying. It was amazing provision at exactly the right time and a powerful lesson in radical giving.

I'm not positive, but I am pretty sure that most of these times of radical provision have been linked with my being provoked by God to give radically— not out of my wealth, but out of my poverty. To give when it hurt, to give when it didn't make sense, to give more than was reasonable— this is what God has called me to do. As I have done so, He has always been faithful to provide. Simply put: you can't out-give God. Period.

I see two very common streams of thought among Christians today when it comes to finances: the "prosperity gospel" and the "spirit of poverty." The more common of the two, the prosperity gospel, teaches that: "God wants you to be happy. He wants to bless you with nice things and wants you to be comfortable." In a nutshell, this ideology says that God wants us to be prosperous. There may be some truth in this; after all, God is the author of blessing. God is good, and He does bless us and provide for us. The problem, however, is that the prosperity gospel completely ignores the countless examples throughout Scrupture of obedient Christians who suffered pain, torture, poverty, and much more. It makes no explanation for the suffering and hardship of people like Joseph, Jeremiah, Job, Paul, the saints of Hebrews 11, and of course— JESUS. Then, conveniently, it ignores the promises which tell us that if we follow Jesus, we are going to encounter hardships and suffering as well.

Over the last several years, certain Christian TV gurus are saying things like: "God wants you to be rich. You're a child of the King. He wants you to prosper." It does not surprise me much to hear this teaching from TV personalities, but I have been quite taken off guard by hearing this prosperity message also infiltrating mainstream Christian churches. I sat and listened to one popular preacher share his testimony about how God enabled his entire family (including his seven year old daughter) to purchase cell phones at half the expected cost. People in the congregation actually started wiping their eyes, touched by the "powerful testimony." It makes me think that many of us mainstream American Christians have allowed ourselves to become a little spiritually deadened, wallowing in our own wealth. Who wouldn't want to hear such a message of ease?

It makes me sick to see this message taught and accepted widely not only in the US, but also around the world. I've sat in many Asian churches and heard it said: "If you trust Jesus, you will have no problems.

God will take care of you, nothing bad will ever happen to you, and He will make you prosperous." That teaching then also works the other way. If calamity hits your family, your Christian brothers and sisters start asking: "What sin were you involved in? What did you do that displeased God?" Where in the world did this kind of thinking come from?

What does this false theology teach us about the countless saints around the world who have suffered, been tortured and martyred, or died in abject poverty while remaining steadfast in their devotion to Jesus? Nothing. Try teaching the prosperity gospel to the saints of the underground church in China, and see how far you get! It doesn't add up. In fact, prosperity theology is a slap in the face to the theology of suffering. Yet it is this— the theology of suffering— that is truly revealed in much of the Scriptures. Sadly, teaching on this topic (and subsequently understanding of it) is largely absent from many mainstream churches.

I remember getting polled a couple of years ago for a denominational magazine. The question was, "What is the biggest thing that you attribute your spiritual growth to over the past few years?" I immediately answered, "suffering and hardship." The interviewer seemed completely surprised. She shared with me that she had interviewed more than 170 people for this article and that, so far, no one had given that answer! Really? Most of them had answered Sunday school, cell groups, Sunday morning sermons, quiet times, and Bible study groups. In our convenience and comfort-centered society, there is very little room for a healthy understanding of suffering.

In addition to the prosperity gospel, there is another school of thought amongst many Christians today regarding wealth. I call it the spirit of poverty, and it may be something they ascribe to without even knowing it. Basically, although it is somewhat hard to define, it's the idea that it's somehow more spiritual to be poor than to be rich. It is a kind of reverse glorification of poverty (real or perceived) because of sacrifice unto the King. Those who hold this belief system walk around in false humility, subtly condemning people who have money and nice things. This idea is, in particular, quite prevalent in the missionary culture.

To be fair, I believe evangelical church culture has, to a degree, taught those in ministry this ideal. I've actually heard people criticize missionaries for some of their lifestyle choices. For example, I overheard one wealthy American man, the father of two children who have been raised with every amenity you can imagine, critiquing a younger missionary family with three children. "Can you believe they bought that nice new SUV? Aren't they living off of support?" It was frustrating. I wanted to shout out, "What? Because they are missionaries living off of support and in full time ministry they are supposed to have a rundown car? What the heck?" This Christian man gave his children every luxury that money could buy. Yet when he saw a missionary family making a big purchase, he condemned them. This should not be. It's a representation of an underlying current of thought which says, "If you commit to full time ministry, you are supposed to be poor." That's just as ridiculous as the gospel of prosperity.

The spirit of poverty is manifested in several unusual ways, some of which are physical and outward and others which are mental bondage. In the first case, individuals operating with this belief will often commit to unusual levels of denial of some of the God given pleasures of life. I've seen this again and again, and it confuses me. For example, I know a young couple serving in the Ukraine. They refuse to buy anything at full price and refuse to let their kids join their neighborhood friends in activities which require money. They never go on vacation, and they won't even buy a snack on their family's Saturday afternoon walks. Sometimes they fall unintentionally into spiritual pride, thinking to themselves: "We are sacrificing so much for the sake of Christ." Others in bondage to the spirit of poverty are obsessed mentally with money. Just as people who ascribe to the prosperity gospel often like to discuss their purchases, these individuals will tend to talk all the time about how they can't afford this or that. Even worse, they sometimes become conditioned to look at people as sources of money rather than sources of relationship.

The truth is that the bondage to money is the root of both the messages of prosperity and poverty. God wants us to have a healthy understanding of finances. The book which has helped me the most in forming my own understanding of finances is *Money, Possessions, and Eternity* by Randy Alcorn. He argues that we need to understand that our life is but a speck on the timeline of eternity, and he encourages us to live with our hearts and eyes fixed on eternity. Let every financial decision you make be intentional, and let it be focused on eternity!

In order to last the long haul with joy, let me encourage you to live simply, to trust radically, and to give extravagantly. Aim to have a healthy understanding of God's heart towards money. Money, after all, is necessary, and it is not inherently evil. The danger is when our obsession with money pollutes our hearts. I love two things that John Wesley said about money: "Make all you can. Save all you can. Give all you can," and "When I have money, I get rid of it quickly, lest it find a way into my heart." As you head to a life as a global worker, be careful to guard your heart from financial obsession. Believe God for miraculous provision, give generously, and seek to live simply for the sake of the gospel. He is more than sufficient for all of your needs.

Chapter
5

Link Hearts: Giving Yourself Away in True Community

"They devoted themselves to the apostles' teaching and to the fellowship, to the breaking of bread and to prayer. Everyone was filled with awe, and many wonders and miraculous signs were done by the apostles. All the believers were together and had everything in common. Selling their possessions and goods, they gave to anyone as he had need. Every day they continued to meet together in the temple courts. They broke bread in their homes and ate together with glad and sincere hearts, praising God and enjoying the favor of all the people. And the Lord added to their number daily those who were being saved." Acts 2:42-47

I THINK THE DAYS OF THE LONE-RANGER missionary are over (knowing full-well that I was in that category in the beginning). I really believe that God wants to use communities in mission. Ideally, you will be able to link up with this kind of community to serve alongside in cross-cultural ministry. Even if you're in a place where this kind of community seems difficult or impossible, you still don't want to do ministry alone. Thanks to the wonders of modern communication, community can be developed and maintained no matter where you are— even on different continents!

It is vital that you link up with friends in life-giving community. These are the kind of friends to whom you can pour out your heart, weaknesses, and insecurities, and who will speak life and encouragement into you. Seek to link up with true brothers and sisters who will be a part of your life forever. "Doing community" isn't necessarily natural for all of us, but I believe it's one of the keys to lasting the long haul in cross-cultural ministry. In true community, such as that described in Acts 2, we lack nothing. God's design for community is that we would be so connected to one another that when one of us is in need— physical, spiritual, emotional or otherwise— the rest of us act quickly to meet that need. We will be so connected in life that we know when another brother or sister has needs before they even have to ask. It really is possible, even for someone living halfway across the world! Several people asked me to talk about support-raising in this book. I laughed out loud and said: "I can't. I don't know anything about it!" While we've had continual miracles of provision over the years surrounding our ministry, I also recognize that a lot of that provision has come from my community. God has given me grace to "do community" well, and one of the indirect fruits of such grace is that our community cares for us and meets our needs.

Before you set out overseas, it is crucial that you have a strong relationship base in your home country. You need a community of people back home who are praying for you, with whom you are in regular contact, and who you know will back you up whenever you need it. If you don't have this right now, then start praying! Reach out and try to link up with people with similar hearts for God. I can't tell you how many times I have heard people who are preparing for full-time ministry complain that they don't have community. Reach out, make friends, and take tangible real steps to connect with other believers now. Don't expect everyone else to make the first steps! Make those steps yourself, and be open to God bringing new friends into your life.

As a brand new Christian, many of my drinking and partying friends rejected me. So I just began praying and seeking to meet new people. "Lord, could you give me some friends? I have no family, and many of my friends don't want anything to do with me. I need you to come through."Literally, within days, people began walking up to me saying things like, "Carissa, let's hang out, we want to be friends with you." I was dumbfounded. These people are still my friends today. Many of them have visited me in Asia, and many support me financially. I am blessed.

So, pray for friends and take steps to reach out and meet people. When you do, though, make sure that you open yourself up for *true* friendship. We all need honest, transparent, real friendships which seek to build up, encourage, and challenge us in our walks with Jesus. You need friends who can help you when needed, and you need to be willing to ask for that help if you need it. It's not a sign of weakness to admit you feel overwhelmed or discouraged! Nor is it a sign that your calling is over if you have a bad day, bad week, or even a bad month. We must be willing to share the good, bad, and the ugly of our lives with each other.

As a relatively new Christian, I felt overwhelmed with a sense of loss in not having any family connections. At the time, I did not understand the strength that Christian friendships can hold. Early one Easter morning, when I was at the sunrise service at church, I remember battling and praying through strong feelings of discontent. Then the Lord spoke to me very clearly about this.

"Carissa," He said, "the blood of the Lamb flows thicker than the blood of this world." At that moment, something changed in my heart, and I started truly appreciating relationships with my brothers and sisters in Christ. I value my family in Christ so much now, and I am quite certain that I would not have made it here for more than twelve years without their support!

Community may come through individuals, but that is not enough. No matter what you may think about it, you need the backing of a church. You need the relationships, support, and community that a church offers. I would even go so far as to say not to go overseas if you don't have this. So do whatever it takes to make it happen!

There are awesome churches all over America. When I hear Christians say things like, "I love that church, but it's a twenty minute drive," I literally want to scream. "Are you kidding? I would drive two hours away to find a life-giving church anywhere around me in Asia." Don't behave like a spiritually spoiled believer. Find a good church, get plugged in, get out of your comfort zone, make friends, show up often, serve, and get connected. You are going to need those relationships back home when you are involved in cross-cultural ministry. If you have a choice to head into ministry now, backed by very little community, or to leave in two years, backed by a strong community, you need to leave in two years. Period. Get connected. You *will* need those support and friendships in the season to come!

I have a number of friends who would literally do anything for me, and I have a home church that totally backs me up. They pray for me. They know what's going on in my life and in my heart. They don't take from me, but rather they seek out ways in which they can care for me. When I struggled with the decision to take a sabbatical, I was able to write to a group of them and ask for help, advice, and direction. When I have emergencies overseas, I can send out an email and instantly have two hundred people praying for me. When I underwent risky emergency surgery, my church immediately sprang into action by paying for and flying over two friends to help me through it. Get connected.

I want to address a very common complaint I hear from missionaries regarding home community and communication. Often, missionaries feel loved and connected for their first month or two or three in ministry. Then the emails start to drop off, the phone calls drop off, and care packages come less often. The "outta sight— outta mind" scenario comes into play, and this happens around the same time the missionaries are hitting more culture shock. Within months, they become angry and disappointed, saying things like: "everyone has forgotten us," or "we feel totally alone out here." They feel forgotten by their own churches, friends, communities, and even families back home.

Thankfully, I learned something early on. I started to realize that the world isn't centered around me! These friends, churches, and communities have a lot going on in their own lives, and relationship is a two way street. It's up to us as missionaries to communicate well and to communicate often. We need to seek to be connected. It's not someone else's responsibility to make sure we are happy and connected— it's our own. Could the American Church do a better job at missionary care? Yes, of course they could. When I watch missionaries struggle with feeling unconnected, though, and starting to become bitter, my word to them is usually: "what are *you* doing to foster relationships? Are you setting up times to Skype? To talk? To email? To call? Are you letting them know what's going on in your life? Do you know what is going on in their lives? Are you a faithful friend? Are you doing all you can to stay connected with your home community? When you go back, do you make efforts to meet up with people, sharing your heart and hearing theirs?"

Please have realistic expectations for your home church. Don't make the mistake of equating a relationship with the senior pastor as relationship with the church! The *people* are the church. Foster relationships with those people! Missionaries often make the mistake of resenting their senior pastor not being intimately involved in their ministry. Be realistic. Is it really fair to expect your senior pastor to be personally involved with every single ministry flowing out of his church? Most pastors have quite a lot on their plates and plenty of unrealistic expectations from people in their congregation already. Recognize that when I talk about relationship with your home church, that is exactly what I mean— relationship with believers in your *church family*. Before you head out, examine your own relationship with members of your church, community, and family. Take steps to get rid of unhealthy and unrealistic expectations that you might have unknowingly placed on them.

Many missionaries are conditioned to look at friends as supporters. They have an agenda when they speak at churches, and they have an agenda when they go out to eat with friends in America. They are conditioned to look at people as sources of income, support, and money. I'm so grateful for the way God has led me to not make our needs known or to ask for funds, for it brings me great freedom. When I meet with friends, I truly have no other thought in my heart than friendship. When I speak at churches, I have no mixed motives. I whole-heartedly believe that the body of Christ needs to step up and give extravagantly to seeing the great commandment and commission fulfilled, but no one wants to be seen as simply a source of money or support. Don't treat them that way!

Community at home is vital, but also ask God for life-giving community with those from your home culture where you live. This may not be easy to find depending on where you serve. I've prayed for such friends off and on throughout the years, and there have been seasons when I was blessed to have life-giving friendships with Americans in Asia. There have also been seasons when I was utterly alone. God surely meets us in our seasons of loneliness, teaching us reliance on Him. I want to be praying for and open to any friendships God gives me, though, making time and room to strengthen such relationships whenever possible. This year, I realized that I needed to open up my home to other Americans living in the area. So I started hosting a Wednesday night group, and we just get together to share our hearts, our struggles, our needs, etc. Some nights we play games, and other weeks we watch a movie. Sometimes we just hang out, and other times we gather together for worship and prayer and intercession. It's new, but it's going well. My point is to not just wait for like-minded friends to ring your doorbell. Pray, then go out and make it happen.

Community with believers at home is vital, and finding some kindred hearts from your own culture in your host country is important, too. Finally, the other kind of relationship that you truly need is with friends from your host culture. I love community with Americans (or others from similar Western cultures) when and if I have it, but I am careful to limit my dependence on it. I am thankful, in fact, for the "alone" seasons when I did *not* have this kind of community. They forced me to rely on my Asian brothers and sisters more, moving into deeper levels of friendship with them. Getting refreshed by westerners/people from you own culture is awesome, but I am advocating balance. If you want to last a long time in cross-cultural ministry, you must cultivate rich and deep relationships with people from your host country.

Many mothers in cross-cultural ministry find themselves alienated by staying at home with their little ones while their husbands are out each day. These mothers would fare so much better if they made friendships and relationships with other mothers in the community! In fact, one of the easiest ways to truly enter into another culture is through your own children. What better way is there to learn the language than to be forced to speak it with other moms? What wonderful insight can you gain as you ask your neighbor for ideas on how to settle your sick child's tummy? What incredible friendship can be forged as you raise your children alongside local moms in true community?

I learned the value of friends in my host culture early on in my time in Asia. I became really sick with malaria (the first of many bouts to come!), and I was helpless. My Asian sisters, Lamae and Chai-mai, had to take care of me completely. They took me to the hospital, stayed with me, and, because I had very little money, they even helped pay the hospital bill. I hated it! However, I watched something 'shift' in Lamae and Chai-mai's hearts, as well as in mine. Instead of their looking upon me as a foreign benefactor, they now saw me as a sister. Likewise, I saw them as true sisters! They were so happy and excited to be in a position to help me, and it was a definite turning point in our relationship. It was even worth getting malaria!

Many missionaries tend to see themselves as benefactors: givers of money, givers of wisdom, givers of knowledge, givers of truth. Very few see themselves as receivers. I am so thankful that my mindset changed on this early on. Understanding equality in community with a host culture is not a one-time lesson, though, and I have had to learn and re-learn this lesson several times. More than twelve years later, I can honestly say that some of my best friends in the entire world are my sisters and brothers in Asia. We've had some ups and downs, but true community has been forged in the process.

Please hear me. Take times to cultivate all three of these types of community, for all three are equally important. A home community who backs you up 100% is crucial. Friends from a similar culture to yours living in your host country (if they are there) are a gift. True friends from your host culture are invaluable.

If you want to last the long haul in cross-cultural ministry, make sure you are deeply connected to life-giving relationships at home and abroad. There is an African proverb which says, "If you want to go fast, go alone. If you want to go far, go together." The truth is that you simply cannot do it alone. You need the body of Christ, and you need true, authentic community. You must be honest and transparent with these trusted friends, letting them know when you are hurting, battling loneliness, feeling depressed, or feeling discouraged. Seek out Godly influences whenever possible, and find others who have walked down the same path from whom you can receive advice and counsel. Above all, be honest with God about your heart. He knows it all anyway.

Many "casualties" of cross-cultural ministry seem to have in common a lack of life-giving community. Pray for this community, and seek it out. Give yourselves to it. Fight for it. You will be glad you did, and you will last longer in ministry. Life giving community is one of the secrets to lasting the long haul with joy!

Chapter
6

Be Incarnational:
Embracing Adaptability
and Living in Grace

"*The Word became flesh and blood, and moved into the neighborhood.*" *John 1:25 (The Message)*

―――――――――― ∾ ――――――――――

"*If you've gotten anything at all out of following Christ, if his love has made any difference in your life, if being in a community of the Spirit means anything to you, if you have a heart, if you care— then do me a favor: Agree with each other, love each other, be deep-spirited friends. Don't push your way to the front; don't sweet-talk your way to the top. Put yourself aside, and help others get ahead. Don't be obsessed with getting your own advantage. Forget yourselves long enough to lend a helping hand. Think of yourselves the way Christ Jesus thought of himself. He had equal status with God but didn't think so much of himself that he had to cling to the advantages of that status no matter what. Not at all. When the time came, he set aside the privileges of deity and took on the status of a slave, became human! Having become human, he stayed human. It was an incredibly humbling process. He didn't claim special privileges. Instead, he lived a selfless, obedient life and then died a selfless, obedient death—and the worst kind of death at that— a crucifixion." Phil 2:1-8 (The Message)*

WHEN IT COMES TO CROSS-CULTURAL MINISTRY, I've seen healthy models. I've also seen unhealthy models, and I've seen mixtures of both. I've unfortunately seen a lot of people function ineffectively or leave cross-cultural ministry early, and I have learned a few things in the process. Simply put— those individuals who seek to die to self, embrace the culture, and seek Jesus in all things, will at most times flourish. Those that don't, won't. It's not rocket science.

This can even be true for short-term teams. I used to ask churches and college groups to only bring experienced people to Joy Homes. "Make sure they've been somewhere else first," I would instruct them. After all, Asia is a hard place, right? One team that came to visit changed my rules. Of the ten on the team, nine had never left the country. (I guess they forgot to read my prerequisites). They were quite shocked upon reaching Asia, and I thought to myself, "Ugh, two whole weeks with them, it's going to be so *hard.*" The truth is, though, that they were one of the best teams we have ever had!

They knew nothing, and, more importantly, they knew that they knew nothing. They came as learners: they were broken, enthralled, inquisitive, and teachable. They were, in a word, awesome. During the home's fasting and prayer night, the entire team was overcome at the sight of little five to nine year olds passionately pursuing Jesus. They joined in wholeheartedly, praying and worshiping as they never had before. This team gained so much from their trip, and the truth is that their hearts' postures were a blessing to all of us. I still keep in touch with many of them today.

Contrast that team with another one who came only months later. This team was a seasoned group of world travelers. Some had graduated from Bible college and some from seminary, and they thought they knew it all. They did not come as "learners" at all. After a particularly powerful time of Sunday night fasting and worship, they sat around and dissected the reasons why Christians in certain settings experience greater anointing and/or passion in worship. I felt sick to my stomach. One of our nine year olds, Simla, came over to me, and said: "This team is not at all nice. They don't know how to pray and worship. All they know how to do is talk, talk, talk. Not at all nice." Enough said.

If you are going to thrive in your host culture, you've got to be teachable and ready to learn to adapt. Stop expecting everyone and everything to change to fit you; you've got to learn to change to fit the culture! Asia is about as different from Georgia as you can imagine. *Everything* is different. When I first came, I had an old Asian "squatty potty" as my toilet. A friend, visiting from America, offered to convert it into a western toilet.

I almost said, "For real? Okay, let's do it." On second thought, though, I declined. Why? Don't laugh, but I realized that I needed to change myself to fit the toilet, not to expect the toilet to change to fit me. It may seem like a ridiculous example, but it's true. It was like a revelation to me. If I was going to make it here a long time, it was not my surroundings that needed to change to fit me. I had to change to fit my surroundings— period.

Lifestyle

LEARN TO ADAPT TO THE CULTURE and the people rather than expecting them to adapt to you. I love that I came to Asia with nothing but a backpack! I had to use what Asia offered instead of bringing it all from the US. Many missionary families ship *everything* from the US, and the result is a lifestyle that remains quite typically American. Their food, clothes, belongings, furniture, entertainment, pastimes, church, and more are all 100% American, yet at the same they are trying to reach Asians for Christ. It's no wonder why most Asians think Christianity is a uniquely American religion!

Most people in the world, from Asia to Africa to Central America to the Middle East, have figured out how to thrive in their own environment. Learn from them! You don't have to bring Advil from home; chances are that your country has some alternative. You don't have to bring your own furniture; use what is available in the place where you live. As much as possible, learn how to function in your host culture as your friends in that culture do. Don't focus on ways to make yourself more at home with familiarity. Don't seek to change the culture, but seek to change yourself to *fit* the culture. Challenge yourself to learn how to function as the people in your community do— to truly adapt to your host country. Yet, at the same time, you must learn what you need to live healthily and to be sustainable long term. In other words, you must identify your real needs. Adapt as you might, you can't simply deny your own culture's influence on who you are, how you operate, and your own thought processes. This is a tricky balance, and I don't know if I have found it yet.

In the early days, I probably went too far in trying to adapt to the culture. For example, one day I was offered water which was clearly dirty. I thought to myself, "Well, if it's good enough for this family, then it's good enough for me." Within forty-eight hours, I was hospitalized with severe dysentery. It took me over twelve days to recover. I had been so dogmatic when it came to my lifestyle that it almost killed me. What's more, this has happened more than once! I've softened up over the years and learned to make decisions which aren't as rigid; these have allowed me to last a lot longer here.

For me, I have found that I need my own room and bathroom, a decent mattress, good books, and a good computer. Your needs may be different. You may need yearly exits for two to three weeks to get rest and gain perspective, or you may need a trip to get American cuisine once each week. When I first came, I spent a few hours out alone one day each week. I went to KFC, propped my feet up, and read international magazines. I looked forward to this time each week initially, but as time went by, I found I needed it less and less. Everyone's needs are different, but try to surround yourself with people who hold similar values in regards to lifestyle. It is helpful to support each other in this endeavor to identify with your host culture.

Some mission agencies allow you to ship or bring over large containers full of your belongings, and I understand how it seems to make sense at the time. For example, you don't have to buy new furniture and appliances if you can just bring them from the US. I am not trying to criticize anyone else's choices, but I am asking you to pray carefully about these kinds of decisions. Just because you are allowed to do something doesn't necessarily mean it's the best thing to do! Here's a different suggestion: Why not give away or sell your possessions as you get ready to move? It's an unconventional idea, but it will help you to commit more fully to your new home. Others in your extended community might make different choices than you, but so what? Why not err on the side of adaptability and simplicity?

I've seen some cross-cultural workers make radically different (plush) lifestyle choices. Let's face it: it's much cheaper to live in many parts of the world than it is in the US. The dollar goes a lot further there, and these individuals interpret that as permission to live lavish lifestyles in their host country. They hire personal drivers, gardeners, maids, and cooks. Feelings of conviction are suppressed with phrases like: "Well, we are providing jobs and salaries for the nationals," and "Life is so much harder here, we need these helpers." In some cases (the exception, not the norm), there is a real need for help, and I want to be careful not to make blanket statements. My friends in Nepal both work as doctors and have two small children at home. After much debate, they hired someone to wash their clothes and cook lunch for their family each day. Washing clothes (by hand) is a two-three hour job there, and cooking from scratch takes several hours. The family wanted to experience Nepali cuisine, but their work schedules would not allow for this if they were to cook themselves. So their decision to hire help allowed them to eat Nepali food and also to have more family time. The decision came after much prayer, thoughts, discussion, and honest evaluation. So I am not saying that getting help is absolutely always wrong, but I do advise caution and intentionality.

On my first mission trip as a college student, we went to Guatemala and stayed on a mission compound where several American missionary families lived. We had comfortable housing arrangements and hot water, and we were the guests of honor at several programs and functions. We would go out in the daytime and "do ministry," and occasionally we would eat a Guatemalan meal. Our evenings and nights and mornings were spent eating Americanized food that was served by Guatemalan partners, and we were even served cool drinks from silver trays by Guatemalan workers as we worked. It was bizarre to me. We were spending much of the day behind nine foot walls in a mini-America right in the middle of Guatemala City! I was a brand new Christian at the time, but I knew enough to recognize that I felt uncomfortable. I began processing the experience in terms of my own future decisions, which I think is the best way to protect yourself from landing in this kind of situation. Make decisions before you go about what kind of missionary you are going to be and what kind of lifestyle you are going to have. If you don't make these decisions before you leave, they will often be made for you. I have some friends who live in India that eat Indian food only once or twice a month! They don't know how to eat with their hands as most Indians do, even though they have been in that country for several years. I'm sure they didn't plan for that to happen, but if you don't intentionally make certain decisions, they will be made for you.

Live simply and adapt whenever possible, but also give yourself grace. A few years ago, after nine years in Asia, I bought a sofa-set. After years of sitting on floors, grass mats, bean bags, and plastic chairs, I started noticing many Asian friends with more permanent furniture. That's when I began praying about getting something myself, and thankfully a financial gift made it possible. Honestly, this has made me feel even more at home here. My room is actually comfortable now! Just a couple of months ago, some ex-pats leaving the country gave me a really nice bed and some nice furniture as well as some appliances. I struggled with keeping it and had to pray it through a bit. I don't have any perfectly clear wisdom or advice on these kinds of decisions, other than to start small, go slow, and pray about each choice. The bottom line is not to seek to make your surroundings fit you as much as you fit your surroundings.

I know a girl who lived in Delhi named Jessica. She refused to take the public transportation that the city offered and insisted on only taking paid taxis. Her house, though modest in size, was furnished with the best amenities available. Someone overheard mutual Indian friends criticizing Jessica, saying things like: "She's so rich. What a nice life she lives. She is not fit for our country." Jessica dressed in Indian attire, spoke the language fluently, and even fell in love with an Indian worship leader. Yet she lived an extravagant lifestyle. The man's family refused to give permission for them to pursue a relationship, certain that Jessica would never adjust to life in India with their son.

I have another friend, Stacy, who was determined to live an incarnational life among the poor in Mumbai. She moved into a slum with no running water and no sanitation, and rats were continually found in her one room tenement. She would never buy anything, even after developing gaping blisters on her feet from the poor quality of the one pair of shoes she owned. When friends advised her to spend a little money and purchase some decent shoes, she refused, saying she wanted to identify with the poor. Within eleven months, Stacy was completely burned out. She became very hard on herself, fell into deep depression, and cried a lot. She lived under constant emotional stress and could no longer handle life in Mumbai. When her sending agency came to visit her, they found her in such a pathetic emotional state that they sent her home. Even after quite some time at home, she is still struggling from the after-effects of her life in Mumbai. She's pretty sure she will never return to any kind of ministry again.

Don't go overboard in either of these directions. It isn't important what you have the money to do or buy; it's more important what God will allow you to do or buy. When I first lived in Asia, I slept on a grass mat, surrounded by three lines of insect chalk (as my defense against roaches).Large rodents known as bandicoots would knock at my door, and I had about two buckets of water a day for bathing and flushing my toilet. I am pretty sure I couldn't have lasted twelve years living like that. I have had to slowly pray and make choices about what God would allow me the grace to do. When you make decisions, start simply, but then let God guide you through the process. I can't write up a set of rules when it comes to this kind of thing. Every one of us will need to navigate these issues as we go.

I am advocating balance and sensitivity in processing your lifestyle choices. If you are married, these choices need to be made together. Often, I see husbands who want to live in a radically simple way, but they completely ignore the very real needs of their wives. These women start to feel guilty and "less spiritual" because of their desire to "nest" in their new homes. Husbands, be realistic! Pray and live simply, but don't be ridiculous in your decisions. If you want to last the long haul, you need to start having honest conversations about what both you and your wife need to be sustainable. Don't assume that your wife is being "unspiritual" just because she wants a decent mattress and bed or a kitchen table! One couple in Bangkok was going through a rough spot in their marriage because she wanted to decorate their home. It was going to cost over 400 dollars to get a little bit of furniture, some curtains, and some things to hang on the wall, and her husband thought she was being too materialistic. They already had a bed, a kitchen table, a stove, a small fridge, five plastic chairs, and sheets on the windows. While he spoke and challenged his wife with ideals of simplicity and godliness, he spent 500 dollars to purchase a second-hand motorcycle because it was much faster than waiting on the bus and tuk-tuks. Since they were good friends of mine, I had no qualms about pointing out the inconsistency of this kind of thinking. Thankfully, he listened, and later that week he and his wife went shopping for some home furnishings. Going the distance cross-culturally will require finding a balance between adapting to the culture as much as possible while simultaneously identifying healthy ways to make your lifestyle sustainable.

Living With Joy

IF YOU SEE YOUR *ENTIRE LIFE* in ministry as a gift from God, then your perspective and outlook will show it. As you embrace this truth, I really believe you will receive a significant sense of belonging and joy. Not only that, but for those who are parents, you will likely notice that your kids' attitudes will show it, as well. There is no need to compensate your kids for their "sacrifice or loss" while in cross-cultural ministry. Life engaged in cross-cultural ministry is a GIFT!

I've seen two kind of families engaged in cross-cultural ministry. In the "sacrificial family," members carry within them a sense of loss. They are passionate about Jesus and His call, but they have an underlying heart posture that says, "I'm sacrificing." These families often send their kids the message that they have been asked to give up a lot to leave home and therefore the parents need to make up for their losses. Out of guilt, they buy their son the latest greatest X-BOX 4 or I-Phone or new guitar. These children often have very few friends from their host culture, and too often their main peer groups are other missionary kids. To compensate for their daughters' losses, they send her to America to "escape the hardships of ministry" each year for the three month summer (since she is suffering for the other nine months). Often, these parents seem absolutely surprised that kids cannot cope when they reach the teen years and are miserable most of time.

Contrast this model with the "the adventurous family." These families look at their lives as a treat and a great adventure. They realize that they aren't giving up anything! They sense that they are the truly blessed ones who get to experience and live in different cultures, be world travelers, and have friends from other ethnicities. What a privilege! These parents feel no need to make up for any losses, but rather they emphasize to their children how richly blessed their lives are. They, as a family, celebrate life in cross-cultural ministry with grace and humor. They thrive. I've quite often watched as these children enter their teen years healthy and happy, holding onto joy, with a strong sense of self and a deep understanding of God's love.

To truly walk in the belief that our ministry lives are blessed gifts, our hearts' posture towards the culture, environment, and people to whom we feel called is crucial. The longer I live here in Asia— the longer I give myself to people here— the more comfortable Asia itself becomes. I absolutely love it here! I don't mean that "I love it despite....this and that...." I mean, I absolutely love it, with no strings attached. Even on a bad day (and believe me, I've had more than my share of bad days!) there is nowhere else I would rather live.

I had some friends visit not too long ago, Americans who had lived in Asia for about three or four years. They kept insisting that they loved the local people, but they talked on and on about how much they hated life there overall. They were completely down on the culture, and honestly, I felt offended. I felt like saying: "How can you hate the place, but love the people? How can you criticize the people's culture so strongly and still proclaim to have Christ's love for them?" People and culture are intricately tied together. God loves us in the *context* of our cultures, not "in spite of" them. How can we say we hate India, but love Indians? How can we love Ghanaians, but hate Ghana? It just lacks authenticity to me. If we are to believe and receive our lives in cross-cultural ministry as gifts, we must love the whole package!

Language

ANOTHER KEY TO LONG-TERM SUSTAINABILITY is language acquisition. Some settings make language learning very easy and practical, and many ministries will connect you with language schools. Others will provide you with not only a language school, but also a host family to live with during the initial period of language acquisition (I believe this setting is ideal). Within the growing landscape of cross-cultural ministry, however, there are more and more small, independent groups launching out with no emphasis on language acquisition. I know many missionaries who have served for years without making any sincere attempts to learn the local language. Since English is quickly becoming a mainstay across the world, especially in urban settings, you can get by in many major cities without learning another language. That's just the thing, though: you can "get by," but you can't "thrive." When you even attempt to learn the language of your host country, you show great respect for your sisters and brothers in that culture. As you progress further in the language, you begin picking up jokes, innuendos, and subtleties of that culture. Eventually, you pick up on much more than just the words being spoken and start to feel the emotions behind those words. This enables you to engage and communicate at a real *heart* level.

My own language learning process has oftentimes been a frustrating one. I began my ministry in a city where four main languages were spoken at all times, three of which had different root bases. Since I was working primarily with street kids at the time, I thought it would be good to ask them to teach me. Well, I learned, alright! One day I asked one of the English speaking street kids how to say, "Please don't cheat me. Be honest, charge me the right price." I was fed up with tuk-tuk drivers overcharging me, and I thought that this phrase could prove to be very valuable. So he taught me the phrase, and I learned it well. I learned it very well, and I repeated it several times a day. I had no idea that I had accidentally learned how to curse and use crude language to communicate.

I'll never forget when, a few months later, I was taking a tuk-tuk ride with an Asian sister. The driver tried to overcharge us, and she was about to fight with him.

Wanting to show off my language skills, though, I assured her that I would "handle the situation." I confidently strolled over to the driver and proceeded to tell him in my expert language: "Please don't cheat me. Be honest, charge me the right price." He got angry with me, so I decided to yell it at him to show him how serious I was. "Please don't cheat me! Be honest. Charge me the right price!!" He grew even angrier with me. My Asian sister, clearly disturbed, threw some money his way and dragged me away from the tuk-tuk. She scolded me and said: "Carissa, you just said something really terrible to that man. You offended him." I said, "What do you mean? All I said was 'Please don't cheat me, be honest, and charge me the right price.'" She laughed and said, "No, no, that is not what you said! You said something so terrible I cannot even repeat it. I don't how to say those terrible nasty words in English." Basically, I came to find out that I had told the tuk-tuk driver: "Why are you cheating me, raping me, and stealing my money, you $#@(*!!@ liar!!" The children had taught me "street language," which often involved cursing and sounded rude and crude to almost everyone else. My Asian sisters kindly informed me that I was also using a rough mixture of words from all three languages! The process of unlearning this took me a *while!*

In our children's home, we take in children from many different provinces. Currently, eight languages are represented in the home! For someone like me who finds learning language challenging, this presented a daunting task. Which language do I learn? What about the people in our community who don't speak it? Should I learn to speak all eight languages? If not, how many? Which ones do I focus on? These were hard questions without easy answers. With no language schools nearby, I was overwhelmed. Eventually, I decided to focus on the language which the majority of people in our area spoke. It was the language spoken by the most vulnerable in our area, but it wasn't even a written language in our city! The signs and newspapers were in a completely different language, and I had no real teacher. Two of my coworkers, who hadn't mastered English, tried their best to help instruct me. Often, though, they would argue among themselves about correct pronunciations of the various words and phrases.

Be patient, and understand that there are various levels of language acquisition. The basics oftentimes take years. To begin, surround yourself with people in your host culture who speak the language and practice with them often. Be prepared to make a fool of yourself again and again and again, but watch as your friends take great delight in the fact that you care enough to even try. They will also usually take great joy in helping you sharpen your skills.

Once you grasp the basics, you will be able to carry on simple conversations with the people around you. Don't be lulled into a kind of false confidence in this stage, believing that you have somehow "arrived." There is still much more to learn! You must next learn to communicate and understand emotions in the local language— to communicate your heart. In this stage, you may begin to understand jokes and cultural innuendos. Yet again, don't be lulled into a false confidence. There is still more to come.

The third phase of language learning comes when you actually begin to dream and to think in that language. Because you are capable of processing information in that language, you find it easier to actually think and to pray that way. Not only do you understand emotions, innuendos, subtleties, and jokes in the language, but you may even begin making jokes yourself! How long does it take to reach this level of language proficiency? I'm not sure because I'm not there yet. The important point is to be intentional about learning language. Nothing communicates your desire to share God's heart better than doing it in the heart language of the local people.

The Early Days

THE PROCESS OF ADAPTING does not happen overnight. As you prepare to move, make a decision to commit to the ministry ahead not based on your feelings, but based on your calling. Buy a one-way ticket! What I mean is, try to make that place your true home. My personal advice is that you not leave your host country for at least eighteen months. Doing so will only confuse you and distract you. Stay, and commit to the work. This early process of adapting is difficult: embracing the new, letting go of things, crossing the language barrier, pushing down the culture barrier. Push through it! Don't go back to your own country, even for a one week visit, during that first eighteen month phase.

With modern technology now available in even the most remote places, I also must caution about over-doing it on communication back home during that initial season. Tools which make it possible to keep in touch with loved ones can easily become hindrances to fully embracing the local culture. Limit your time on the internet, phone calls, email, and Skype, for these things can become escape mechanisms. I advise that you make a decision early as to how often and when you will use these tools, and my suggestion is that you limit yourself to one or two times per week in that initial year or two. It will be hard to do, but your adjustment to your host culture will be much faster and healthier as a result! I am amazed at the saints of old who went four to five years at a time with nothing but letters which had to travel over oceans and continents for months! Please be careful. Just because it's available doesn't mean you should overdo it.

You also must be aware of the upcoming culture shock. Historically, almost every missionary hits this phase between their fourth and eleventh month overseas. When a lot of their usual defense and escape mechanisms no longer work, they become testy, discouraged, un-motivated, and frustrated. Some even go through a mild depression. The "romantic" season of missions is over. It's not a matter of questioning your calling; it's not even a matter of praying yourself out of it. It's a physiological response to living in a drastically different culture, and it's inevitable. If someone in cross-cultural ministry says they've never experienced it, they are either lying or in self-denial.

If you leave during this time, it can be catastrophic. I've seen it again and again. Missionaries who leave between the fourth and eleventh month of adaptation, even for a short trip, many times don't recover. Take, for example, the wonderful family who had just begun a four year commitment with a ministry in Cambodia. Although they had committed to four years of ministry, they arrived with round trip tickets so that they could leave in the fifth month. It was "just to attend a family members' wedding." Well, when the time arrived, they were in a mild funk. It was textbook culture shock. When this dear family came back from the wedding, they couldn't seem to get over a sense of discouragement and depression. Because their seventeen day exit had actually intensified their feelings of culture shock, things seemed much worse than when they left. They had a really hard time bouncing back, and they ended up leaving the field after only thirteen months.

Go ahead right now and find your calendar. Mark between months four and eleven after your arrival overseas, and write these words: "You're going through culture shock. It's not a reflection of your walk with Jesus or your call. It's just culture shock. Don't over-spiritualize things. This too shall pass. It's just a season. It's normal. Press in and push through, you will come out of it."

You will definitely go through some highs and lows in the process of adapting. Regardless of how you feel, though, keep trying to push forward. I have two sets of friends here in the city for a two year commitment. One of the couples doesn't want to decorate their home, learn a language, or get too attached. After all, they reason, it's only for two years. The other couple lives simply, decorated their home to make it warm, and has completely gotten attached to all of their community and host culture. They really live here, and they have made this their home. Of the two couples, I am positive the second one will not only be more effective here, but also last longer and experience more joy.

I cannot tell you how many singles, couples, and families that I know who have left their host country early because they were unable to adapt. Many of them had unrealistic expectations for their time in ministry. Many knew it would be hard, but they didn't really expect it to be as hard as it was. If you don't want to join their ranks, I implore you to move to your new home with open eyes. Look for ways to change and fit into your host culture. Your natural human instinct will be defensiveness, and you will want to seek out comforts and conveniences to make your life easier and more familiar. I challenge you to try to do the very opposite of what these natural instincts tell you to do. Jesus gave up all the privileges of being the Son of God in order to walk among us. He gave up everything associated with being the Son of God in order to show us the way. He made himself vulnerable and helpless, and He laid down all His rights in order to reach us. As you head overseas, purpose in your heart to follow His example.

Chapter 7

Know Clearly: Knowing Who You Are and Cultivating a Healthy Identity

"What, then, shall we say in response to this? If God is for us, who can be against us? He who did not spare his own Son, but gave him up for us all—how will he not also, along with him, graciously give us all things? Who will bring any charge against those whom God has chosen? It is God who justifies. Who is he that condemns? Christ Jesus, who died—more than that, who was raised to life—is at the right hand of God and is also interceding for us. Who shall separate us from the love of Christ? Shall trouble or hardship or persecution or famine or nakedness or danger or sword? As it is written: "For your sake we face death all day long; we are considered as sheep to be slaughtered." No,

in all these things we are more than conquerors through him who loved us. For I am convinced that neither death nor life, neither angels nor demons, neither the present nor the future, nor any powers, neither height nor depth, nor anything else in all creation, will be able to separate us from the love of God that is in Christ Jesus our Lord." Romans 8:31-39

WE LIVE IN A WORLD that loves to admire people. We seem to have a strong desire to put certain people up on pedestals, and it's crazy. I'm even guilty of it myself. When I was a new Christian, I went to hear the "famous" Bruce Olsen speak at a conference. I had recently read his book, "Bruchko," and as far as I knew, he was nothing less than a living hero. After the event, we had a chance to talk to him. Someone asked me to take him a cup of juice, but my hand was shaking so badly that I splashed it on the floor. My friend had to take over as I stood there unsure of what to do: I had never been so close to greatness before (ha ha). I was so disappointed when I found out he was just a regular guy.

When others hear of my life in Asia with 48 children, they seem to assume that I am a saint. (Those who know me are laughing out loud. Nothing could be further from the truth!) Within the church culture, though, people tend to look at missionaries as heroes and heroines. So when you enter a life of cross-cultural ministry, people are inevitably going to put you up on a pedestal. What will you do? This kind of idolization can be dangerous because you might actually start believing what they say about you is true. It's happened to me personally, and more than once. You must prayerfully guard yourself against this mentality. Beware of the people who say "wow" when they hear your testimony or stories about your encounters with the Lord. *Don't surround yourself with people who are enamored with you.*

As certainly as there will be those who praise you, there will be others who criticize you. You have to come to a place where neither criticism nor praise pierce your heart— a place defined by your closeness to Jesus. You want to find the place where you are so lost in Him that you don't worry about what others think of you. It's possible! The secret is to learn from the One we follow. When Jesus was preaching in the synagogue in Nazareth, everyone thought he was amazing! (Luke 4) They praised him and were amazed at his gracious words. Moments later, though, the same crowd wanted to kill Him. How did Jesus deal with these extremes of adoration and praise, hatred and anger? I believe the secret is found just before this, in Luke 3. Only days before He preached in Nazareth, Jesus had heard the very voice of His Heavenly Father saying: "This is my Son, in whom I am well pleased!" The secret to having a healthy identity is in knowing how your heavenly Father feels about you.

So as you head towards cross-cultural ministry, you must endeavor to protect your heart and mind from a sense of false identity. One problem with this is that our identity too easily gets mixed up with what we do. Especially in American culture, we constantly emphasize "doing" over "being." Performance is everything— even in the church. We must be careful to stay so deeply grounded and rooted in God that we are able to see the difference between *who we are* and *what we do*. As you head overseas, a key part of this is maintaining a healthy understanding of expectations.

In modern-day America, Martha would be seen as a Godly, hard-working servant, while Mary would be looked down upon as lazy and selfish. I can tell you from my own experience in Asia, Joy Homes was built (in the heavenlies) through a season of my being "Mary." My first few months in Asia were marked by nothing but prayer and waiting, waiting and prayer. Still to this day, the entire ministry is built on this *one thing*: sitting at the feet of Jesus. Ministry and fruit flow naturally and easily from this posture.

I know deeply in my heart that my identity rests in God, not in what I do for Him. Despite that, there have definitely been times when I struggled to walk in that belief. The second time that I came to Asia I was seeking God for direction and insight about what to do next. For several months, all that I could email back home were reports like: "Today I played with some street kids, took a long walk, prayed, read my Bible, took a nap, prayed again, wrote in my journal, took another walk, fed some street kids dinner, and went to bed." By American standards, it was very "unproductive." I remember battling feelings of shame because I hadn't actually "done anything" that day. Today, I'm convinced that Joy Homes was being built in the heavenlies at that very time!

On my first trip to Asia, I volunteered in an orphanage for a few months before I started our home. I knew no one. I had nothing to my name. As I interacted with the children, I fell in love with them. Pretty soon, though, it dawned on me that the kids could care less about all the things I used to find my identity in. The fact that I had a masters degree from seminary meant nothing to them. Who I knew or what movements I was connected with meant nothing to them. My stories of faith and miracles and my radical testimony meant nothing to them. My American personality and sense of humor meant nothing to them. As I realized this, something started to happen in my heart. I grew uneasy, uncomfortable, and discontent, and all kinds of ugly feelings came to the top of my heart. It was a bittersweet time for me. Everything I thought that I was, was shaken and broken (that was the bitter part). What was left standing was me alone clinging to the cross (that was the sweet part). God did a powerful work in my heart during that season which has stayed with me for life.

Inevitably, when your comforts, defenses, and escape mechanisms are taken away from you, you will come face to face with your own darkness. Your false identity will be stripped away, and any kind of stripping is bound to be painful. The good news is that if you embrace Jesus in this season, you will have a healthier identity in the long run. The bad news is that you will probably go through many seasons of this problem in your life with Christ: it's not a one-time thing. Let me encourage you that He is worth it!! The treasures He wants to put within you are immeasurable if you will embrace Him during these seasons!

Jesus has now grounded and rooted my identity so firmly in Him that I can truly say I see myself completely separate from what I do. When I go to God, it's as His daughter, His friend, His sister, and His beloved. It has nothing to do with my ministry or mission at all. It may all be taken away from me tomorrow. If it is, I will be shaken— but I won't be destroyed. I won't be devastated, and I won't be hopeless or despondent. Joy Homes is what I do, it's *not* who I am. I am His— simply His.

I have not always understood this so well. I had a heart-changing encounter with God, though, soon after my first trip to Asia. When I returned from that initial trip, I walked away with some pretty negative thoughts. Politically, socially, economically, and spiritually, darkness seemed to permeate the whole area. The poverty was unlike anything I'd ever seen, with hundreds of squatter homes, people living on the streets, non-stop beggars, and street children everywhere. Hopelessness prevailed. I was confident that Christ was the answer to it all, but I wasn't sure *how* He was the answer. If I had previously held any "romantic" notions of being a missionary, they were promptly dispelled by that trip. The implications were profound.

I remember my prayers during that trip. "Lord, I don't really even like this region. It is too hard, yet I feel Your call here. To tell you the truth, I don't think I will be able to make it here. Lord, I know that human pity or human compassion won't last long here. If this is where you want me, then I pray— give me your heart for Asia!" I stood praying over a map of Asia, and I began pleading with God for His heart for the area. Then as I prayed, I heard God clearly say to me: "How can I give you my heart for Asia, when you don't even know my heart for you?"

"Oh no, God," I argued. "You don't understand. I want Your heart for Asia. I didn't come here for me. I just want your heart for Asia."

Again, He told me: "How can I give you My heart for Asia, when you don't even know My heart for you?" I was undone.

During that initial trip, God began to pour out His love for me in fresh new ways. Since the beginning of my walk with Christ, I had known in my *mind* that Jesus loved me. During three years of seminary, the Lord had revealed more of His love for me in my *heart*. During this time, though, God revealed the depth of His love for me in my *spirit*. He began pouring out His love in a new measure, and I experienced it in the innermost part of my being. I heard His songs of love over me in the depths of my soul. Zephaniah 3:17 tells us that:

"The Lord your God is with you. He is mighty to save. He will take great delight in you. He will quiet you with His love. He will rejoice over you with singing."

To understand that Jesus loves us is a good thing. To know this love in our hearts is an awesome thing. To experience the depth of His love in our very *spirit*— this is the thing that will set us free!

As I started out praying for God's heart for Asia, He revealed the depth of His heart for me. Then, *because* of this incredible truth, He actually started giving me the very thing I had asked for: His heart for Asia! Even as I write this, my heart stirs within me. It is because of His great love for me that I am enabled to go and love others. While I certainly did not have a whole lot of "success stories" from that first short time in Asia, I knew God much more deeply than I did before I went. That experience prepared me for His call on my life.

Even if you learn this lesson once, you will probably have to re-learn it several times. I certainly have. Just a few years ago, in 2008, I sent out this email:

> Have had a tough couple of weeks. A lot to share, and I don't even know where to begin. What do I say? What do I omit? Is there such a thing as being too transparent?
>
> Let me just say this, we have had a tough few weeks. Have had to make some hard decisions. Have had to press into God to even hear Him. Have had to care for sweet little Tasanee as she has begun a heavy dose of HIV drugs (with frustrating side-effects). Have had to deal with issues at the kids' school. The hardest thing of all was having to let go of two of our boys this week. To make my outlook even worse, I am sick this week, feeling less than 100% physically, which adds to the complications.
>
> I have noticed a significant lack of patience this past two weeks. A subtle hardening of my heart. I don't feel burnt out or emotionally wrecked, but just noticing a shift in my heart, and I don't like it. So...I have been praying. And I realize that somehow in the past few weeks, I have actually done the very thing I warn others never to do. I have gone to God with a misplaced identity.
>
> I have shared messages about how crucial it is to realize that our identity has nothing to do with "external circumstances", "what we do", "our ministry", "our successes", "our failures", etc... It is completely other than those things. Our identity is completely separate than

all of these things. When I encounter God, it is pretty simple. I am His Beloved, a child, a daughter, friend. He sees me and relates to me as such. I know this. I know this. I know this. I know this. Come on, Carissa.....I teach others about it, for crying out loud.

What happened? I had a tough few weeks in a row, and our home honestly had a tough few weeks in a row, and somewhere along the way, I actually started seeing my identity and relationship with Him as somehow wrapped up in Joy Homes, the kids, etc... What?? When the home took a hit, I personally took a hit too. When the home experienced some failures (or perceived failures), I experienced them personally. I have been able to separate these kind of things in the past, but these days, it has become muddled.

So......I came to this realization when I sat down to spend time with God the other day, and I immediately began praying through the different things that had happened in Joy Homes. I came to encounter God for me personally, I need a lot of HIM, I think I might be more needy than most. Ha.

So, I came with this huge weight/burdens of some of the hard stuff Joy Homes is going through. And I began praying........I was praying for Tasanee (my youngest one—HIV +) at first. And I heard God actually tell me to stop praying for her. (What?? does that make any sense?) Literally, I heard God say, "Carissa, Stop praying for her. Stop it. That's not why I brought her to you. Others are praying for Tasanee. She's a gift to you. *It's not your job to pray for her, it's your job to ENJOY her.*

What?? I couldn't believe it. I started crying, weeping actually. And I felt my heart begin to soften. I began praying for the other issues, the two boys that left, some other problems, etc... And I again felt like

God chastised me gently. "What are you doing? I can barely recognize you with all that you are dressed in."

I knew, at that moment, exactly what was wrong. I was relating to God in terms of Joy Homes, the ministry, my role, etc... I usually am pretty careful about that, but it just slipped in. This dangerous (seemingly innocent) way of relating to God. I was dressed in another identity. I was relating to God through a false identity. In terms of what I do, how others see me, or my ministry.

I have known friends who are involved in ministry, and you ask them, "Hey, how's it going? What's God doing in you these days? What's he teaching you? How's your heart?" And they answer..... "Well, the church is growing, we have 20 more members," or "Our ministry is thriving," or "Our ministry is struggling," etc... And I am thinking, "What?? I didn't ask you about your ministry, I asked you about YOU." See, their identity is SO WRAPPED UP IN WHAT THEY DO.

Such a dangerous thought will inevitably show up in our prayer lives. We actually began to think that God relates to us based on our performance or anointing. If you had asked me how I was doing a week ago, ugh! I would have told you about Joy Homes. Thank you Jesus, that You reminded me.....He reminded me that my walk with Him, that my relationship has nothing to do with what others think of me, my anointing (or lack of anointing), my ministry, the ministry's successes or failures, my self-image, my emotions, external events or circumstances.......... My relationship with God is completely SEPARATE THAN.......all of these things. And that, guys, is great news!! When I think of some of my best friends, the ones I enjoy hanging out with the most, I realize that we have a deep friendship that has very little to do with the hype surrounding my life. And vice-versa. They know me, the good, the bad, the ugly, and they think I am awesome anyway!

So, I sit today enjoying God as a friend. We are hanging out. Has nothing to do with ANYTHING except this: I am His. I am crazy about Him. He is my Hope. My Fire. My Strength. My Passion. My Life. (My heart is softening.) And the cool thing is that He thinks the same thing about me. Not based on ALL OF THIS HYPE (Joy Homes), but based on relationship. He knows me. The Good, The Bad, The Ugly, and He thinks I am awesome anyway. Ha. Good news indeed.

If all of this (my life in Asia) were to fall away, I would still stand. My identity with Christ would not be wrecked. It has very little to do with my life in Asia. Please.....know this. Your identity with God is completely *separate than* your ministry, your works, etc.....

Go....hang out with God. Let him peel away the false identities, and let Him speak to you, give you a pure and perfect identity. If your heart is subtly getting hard, let Him soften it. Both of you will be glad you did.

As MANY OF YOU GET READY to head to full time ministry, I have a strong desire to speak these words of life into you: "You are loved *deeply* by God. There is *nothing* you can do to make Him love you more! God wants your heart! He is pleased with you because you are *His*. There is nothing you can do to make him love you less! He loves you to the fullest!" I long for each of you to know the depths of God's heart for you.

True ministry comes from being with Jesus: everything else will flow out of that. The more we spend time in His presence, receiving His love, the more we will be able to go and share that love with the world. If I challenge you in one way, let it be this: *before you can have God's heart for others, you must know His heart for you.* He loves you with a relentless love. Let Him speak His words of love into your spirit.

If you are going to thrive in cross-cultural ministry, guard your heart against any kind of false identity placed on you by the world. Consider who you were apart from Christ, but dwell on who you now are in Him. Know God's heart for you apart from what you do— His endless, amazing, passionate love for you. It is then that you will know who you truly are.

Chapter
8

Discern Well:
De-mystifying the Call
and Hearing God's Voice

"The man brought me back to the entrance of the temple, and I saw water coming out from under the threshold of the temple toward the east... As the man went eastward with a measuring line in his hand, he measured off a thousand cubits and then led me through water that was ankle-deep. He measured off another thousand cubits and led me through water that was knee-deep. He measured off another thousand and led me through water that was up to the waist. He measured off another thousand, but now it was a river that I could not cross, because the water had risen and was deep enough to swim in—a river that no one could cross...so where the river flows everything will live."
Ezekiel 47:1, 3-5, 9

THIS CHAPTER IS WRITTEN to address the mysterious notion of the "call" to cross-cultural ministry. Christians, for years, have done a great job of romanticizing "the call." It's so idealized, in fact, that many have envisioned a great golden phone, that one day—*if* you are *chosen*—might just ring for you, too. You might get *the call*.

I want to spend just a moment de-mystifying this mysterious call. Does God speak through visions, signs, and wonders, and prophetic words? Of course He does, and often. The danger in many circles, though, is that many are waiting for some kind of supernatural writing in the sky to appear. "GO TO X-COUNTRY," they expect it to say, and it must be seen before the individual takes any steps anywhere. Many people actually have a stirring in their hearts to give their lives away, but they are crippled because they are always waiting for this call. Meanwhile, God is moving, speaking, and stirring in their hearts. They are simply unable to recognize His voice because of this unrealistic waiting on a "golden phone call from God."

I know many people who have a desire to do radical things in the Kingdom of God, yet they hesitate because they aren't sure if they've been called. I have a friend who loves Jesus, for example, who really wants to live in Manila making Christ known to street children. Yet she just waits and waits on the mysterious call, and she hasn't taken any steps towards getting prepared. I've shared with her my impressions: "Do you think YOU were good enough to come up with such an idea? God put that idea in your heart....He wants to fulfill it!"

So many Christians have deep stirrings from God. They feel God calling them towards a life of full time cross-cultural ministry, but they are paralyzed with fear: fear of making the wrong decision, fear of failure, fear of commitment. They view God's will as a great mystery or, worse yet, a dangerous tightrope over a raging river. In this viewpoint, they must always be careful not to fall off of the dangerous line into the rushing river below. However, God's will is not that tightrope! When Christians hesitate trying to balance on an impossible, invisible tight rope of God's will and His call, they miss the truth that the river— the river of the Holy Spirit— is the will of God. More explicitly, His will is found in that deep, deep part of the river where the current is the strongest and the water is bottomless. Too many stand idly by, wading only ankle or knee deep in the river, sadly remaining too timid and unable to dive in. I would personally rather jump into the river of His Presence, miss the mark entirely, and trust His current to carry me to the right place than never to jump in at all! There's nothing sadder to me than a wasted life.

That being said, I truly believe that as we abide in Christ, God puts hints of our destiny within us. He doesn't set us out on a wild goose chase to figure out what we are supposed to do: He actually deposits a sense of our own destiny in our hearts. The more clearly we know God, the more clearly we will see. Where in the world did we get the idea that God cloaks His will for our lives behind smoke screens and buries it amongst hidden clues?

One way I teach my children to understand Scripture is to grapple with Bible verses by putting them into their own words. One day, I asked them to paraphrase, in Joy Homes English, the verse Psalm 37:4: *"Delight yourself in the LORD and He will give you the desires of your heart.*" Here is the way that eleven year old Simla paraphrased it: "If you keep being happy with Jesus only, then He will put things in your heart to do and be and see, and then He will do those things." It reminds me of when we bought the children in our home new bikes for Christmas. The children had never asked for a bike or even shown any interest. But we found some bikes that were cute and on sale, so we secretly purchased six of them for the kids to share. We hid them well. Then, over the next month until Christmas, we kept making subtle comments:

"Wow, look at that kids' bike, it's so cool."

"Wish we had some bikes, it would be so fun to ride them everywhere."

I would tear out a picture of a kid riding a bike and leave it on the table where my kids would eye it when they passed by. Within three weeks, every single child between the ages of seven and ten were convinced that there was nothing they wanted in the whole world more than bicycles! SO....on Christmas morning, they got their hearts' desire! We planted that desire into their hearts so that it became their desire as well, and then we fulfilled it.

While God may very well have put within you a sense of a certain destiny and call, this is sometimes mystified to an extreme. It is commonly taught that calling is some-how tied to a place, a people, or a job, and people feel crippled if they don't know all the details of their par-ticular "call." I think we have it wrong. God taught me early on in my time in Asia that my absolute primary calling is to know Jesus. Everything else, the details, the place, the who, what, when, and how is just context, it's your assignment. Your context and assignment may change, but your calling never will.

It's hard to wrap our minds around this because so many of us have been taught that our "calling" is focused on a place, time, people group, nation, etc. I think that we desperately need a new understanding of our HIGHEST and TRUEST call: to know Jesus. Period. Paul said in Philippians 3:7-8:

"But whatever was to my profit I now consider loss for the sake of Christ. What is more, I consider everything a loss compared to the surpassing greatness of knowing Christ Jesus my Lord, for whose sake I have lost all things. I consider them rubbish, that I may gain Christ and be found in him."

Let me quote one of my boys, Kenye, who brilliantly paraphrased this into Joy Homes English a few years ago: "Everything else is complete waste of time. The only thing that matters is knowing Jesus. Everything else is dirty trash, compared to knowing Jesus and being completely with Him."

Many cross-cultural workers sense God leading them to return home, but along with that comes a sense of failure. I want to say to them: "No Way! Are you kidding? How can it be a failure to listen to God? As long as you pursue this beautiful man, Jesus, then the rest will fall into place. God is after your heart!" The calling never changes, but the context does. I truly believe my own calling has nothing to do with Joy Homes or this country or these children. My calling is completely other than these things. My first call is to pursue Jesus, to love Him well, and to receive His Love for me. Asia, Joy Homes, the children.....it's all context.

I had a friend return home early to pursue God in the next step in her life (marriage), but some told her that she was being disobedient to her calling to Asia by leaving early. I think the basic premise from which they were operating was wrong. Her journey with the Lord was progressing, but the context and circumstances around that were changing. I sincerely believe that she was right in the middle of His will in choosing to "return home early." She actually returned to Asia later with her husband to serve at Joy Homes for another two years! The main point is just to be grounded in knowing Jesus so intimately that you can go wherever He leads in a moment. The "how, when, who, where, what" isn't the main thing: knowing Him is the main thing. Your context and assignment may change throughout your life, but the calling never will.

Since we are in the business of dispelling myths about the "call," let's work on one more. It has to do with meeting needs. I've seen missionaries burning out again and again because they believe their call is to meet all needs, but they can't possibly meet all the needs around them. Their ministry becomes powerless to help anyone because they are too overwhelmed and exhausted with trying to help everyone.

Another truth I learned early on (and have had to re-learn several times since) is that the "need" is not the same as "the call." The call is the call. Period. Let us get this truth into our hearts. There will always be needs pressing into us on every side. We've got to get to a place of walking so closely with Jesus that we are able to discern which needs He actually intends for us to meet and to guard our hearts against pressure to meet those He doesn't. We must be able to hear His voice: "*Whether you turn to the right or to the left, your ears will hear a voice behind you, saying, 'This is the way; walk in it.'*" (Isaiah 30:21)

I am convinced that if we don't get this principle deep into our hearts, we will be overwhelmed by the vast needs that surround us. If we carried out the assumption that "the need is the call," we would have to move to the poorest people group in the poorest country in the hardest part of the world. We should, by default, go where the need is greatest, right? Currently, in 2011, that would either be Haiti, North Korea, or Burma. So every Christian must drop what he or she is doing and head to one of these three places if the need is the call. The needs of the world, however, are *not* the call.....*Jesus* is the *call*. I am thankful I learned this early on, or I wouldn't have 48 children: I would have 4800! I would also be overwhelmed, exhausted, ineffective, and powerless. We can't let our emotions rule us: we must be ruled by the Spirit of God. The only way to walk in this reality is to cultivate a deep inner walk with the Lord.

As you get ready to head towards cross-cultural ministry, go with a healthy grasp on this notion of "calling." First of all, remember that it is not some unattainable, mystical thing: God has already put hints of His destiny inside of you. The only reason why we have missionary heroes is because there aren't enough of us living out our destinies! If we would obey and do that which God has called us to do, there would be a lot less heroes. Everyone would simply be doing what they were created to do. Nobody would know your name, but the world would know the name of Jesus!

Secondly, remember that your biggest calling, superseding all others, is simply to know Jesus and worship Him forever. The ultimate call is to know Him and love Him well. The circumstances and surroundings for that are all just context, and so are the needs that will surround you. You must have an intimate walk with Christ and hear His voice on a daily basis in order to discern which of those needs you are supposed to meet. If you want to thrive in cross-cultural ministry, it is important to de-mystify this sense of "calling." Set yourself on the path towards knowing Jesus more intimately, and you will know your *true* calling!

Chapter
9

Rest Deeply: Discovering the Secret of Sabbath Rest

"Come to me, all you who are weary and burdened, and I will give you rest. Take my yoke upon you and learn from me, for I am gentle and humble in heart, and you will find rest for your souls. For my yoke is easy and my burden is light."
Matthew 11: 28-30

"There remains, then, a Sabbath-rest for the people of God; for anyone who enters God's rest also rests from his own work, just as God did from his. Let us, therefore, make every effort to enter that rest, so that no one will fall by following their example of disobedience." Hebrews 4:9-11

FOR YEARS, I COULD LOOK AT MISSIONARIES and people in full time ministry and spot burn out or weariness or exhaustion a mile away. Working oneself to death seemed to be the norm, not the exception. When our pastor in Asia was hospitalized for "unknown causes," I sat with him for two hours as we talked about the importance of Sabbath rest.

Do you remember how I mentioned in the introduction that I was just beginning to live out some of the truths in this book? Well, after almost twelve years in Asia, I am on my first sabbatical. I am currently at the beginning of the third month of a six month break. While I have always seen the value for other missionaries in taking a Sabbath rest, I thought it didn't apply to me. After all, I've virtually adopted nearly fifty children and become their surrogate mom. What mom takes a Sabbatical? I have come to see myself not as a missionary, but rather as someone who just loves Jesus, loves children, and loves Asia. With that self-awareness, I thought that a three week break every other year or two was more than enough. Thankfully, God got through to me in my stubbornness, and convinced me I needed to take a long break. I needed to rest physically, to get renewed spiritually, and to get revived emotionally. I can't say it's been easy, but I know it is what God wants.

When I talk about Sabbath rest, I'm not just talking about sabbaticals and furloughs. I'm also talking about the rhythm of daily life that we find with Jesus when we walk in steady union with Him. It's the place where we find rest in each day. It's where we set aside time each day not only to pray/worship/read, but also just to rest in His presence. I'm talking about a *divine rhythm* with

Jesus that is undeniable— a source of strength and grace and peace that supersedes every circumstance. Is it even possible?

In our children's home in Asia, we rely on a bore well in our backyard for our daily supply of water. Well, one day we turned on the faucets to find nothing but brown water dripping slowly from the tap. Ugh. Fifty kids, twelve adults, and no water. Not fun, right? We called someone to repair it, and he proceeded to pull out the piping— all 180 feet of it. This came right up out of the ground, winding its way throughout our backyard.

This guy was reputable, and he explained to us that he would require a bore well digger to go deeper. We had exhausted the water supply levels, and we would need to drill deeper in order to get more water. There apparently was a huge clear, clean reservoir of water about another 120 feet down. The big problem was that his estimate was over $2,500 USD. In Asia, that is a ton of money (50% of what it costs to run our entire home per month!) This was not good news: a lot of money and at least a week without water. A second "expert" diagnosis was similar.

As we started working out how to pay for this endeavor, on a whim, we decided to get one more opinion. So we called another man, told him the problem, and within an hour he had found the real source of the issue. He said, "Madam, you do not need to go deeper— you need to take care of your motor. The problem isn't with your depth, it's with the condition of your motor. You are not giving it enough rest in between cycles. You are overusing the motor and not maintaining it." The harsh weather and climate had worn down the motor parts, and they were rusty from lack of care.

So we had not been giving our motor enough rest in between water pumping cycles, nor had we been performing proper maintenance. As a result, it was overused and under-maintained. A few worn out, rusty parts were replaced, and he added some oil here and there. The problem was fixed within two hours, and he proceeded to put the 180 feet of pipe back in the ground. Soon we had crystal clear water gushing out again, all for the total cost of $220.00 (not $2,500!) After more than a week without water, we were truly thankful!

As I processed this, I had a major revelation. Previously, whenever I had hit a wall (whenever things got overwhelming), I always assumed that the answer was to pray more, fast more, and to "dig deeper." I interpreted roadblocks and obstacles of any kind as a call to go deeper and get more radical with God. I frequently mistook my weariness and exhaustion as simply a need for more prayer, but honestly, it didn't really work (at least not for long). This well incident brought huge revelation to me: I was missing it!

God reminded me of my need for intentional rest in Him. He cautioned me against burn out with a very real reminder that the 'elements' around me can wear me down fast. The answer is not always my pushing myself to go deeper, but rather a matter of my resting between cycles and getting my motor and pump serviced. I felt a clear beckoning from the Lord: "Come and rest with Me and in Me. Let Me give you what you really need. Let Me protect you from the elements, clean you up, remove the dirt, pour oil on the rusty parts, so that you can receive all that I have for you." The source is easily within reach, but we need to be healthy as we learn how to tap into it! All of us can live without shelter, food, and electricity for a period of time, but we can't survive without water. It is *life*. The spiritual parallel here is undeniable.

I've realized during the course of writing this book that many people heading into full time ministry are looking for healthy models from whom they can learn. There are many great models out there of powerful, life-giving ministry, prayer, and emotional health. We don't often see a lot of people in ministry modeling Sabbath rest, though. Truthfully, I don't know many at all. Most of us are running full-steam ahead at 110%, and we dismiss our weariness and exhaustion as necessary and normal. Others try to over-spiritualize it with comments about the "true price of discipleship" or "there will be time to rest in Heaven." Jesus rested often. Apparently, according to statements like these, some of us are better off than Jesus.

Daily Sabbath

I HAVE IDENTIFIED three different kinds of Sabbath rest. The first one is the kind of rest that is birthed out of a rich personal devotional life with God. He loves to spend time with us individually, in a secret place. We were made for this! I'm not talking about a legalistic "quiet time," but rather a significant amount of time each day set aside to cultivate a rich relational life with Jesus. What I am envisioning is a time set aside each day where I can go and pour out my heart to God. It is a time when I can read and meditate on God's word, and a place where worship music washes over my soul. It is the place in my heart where I can listen and wait as I sit before Him at His feet.

When I counsel believers, one of the questions I love to ask is: "Tell me about your secret life with God?" Many of them get flustered, and feelings of shame blanket their face as they hang their heads down. Many people seem to have very little concept of spending such intimate time with Jesus. Once, however, I discovered someone who very much understood this idea, and she was living it out in deep communion with God. This young seminary student asked me to speak into her life and to challenge her to go to the next level with God. So, as I often do, I asked her: "Tell me about your times alone with God." She got this excited look on her face and said: "Well, earlier this week, I just felt His presence. I closed my door and locked it, lit a candle, and got my Bible and journal out. I sat on the floor of my dorm room and just waited. In what seemed like minutes, I felt the joy of Jesus invade my heart. My heart was beating wildly, as I was completely overwhelmed with the goodness of God. I thought I might die, it was so strong. He began speaking truth into my heart about His feelings for me and my destiny. I couldn't even talk! I remember just thinking to myself, 'Is this what true love feels like? Is this what true love feels like? It's unbearably good.' I was overwhelmed with joy. I lifted my head up and saw that the candle was almost burned out. I had been there for more than three hours!" This young seminary woman didn't really need my advice or counsel; she had found out the secret of a rich life with Jesus.

What happens in these moments of daily rest is that we begin to let God point out the areas of our hearts and lives that don't align with His. We also begin to understand and feel the things that make His heart beat faster, the things in which He delights. God begins to share with us the secrets of His heart! He opens up the Bible to us so it actually becomes the word of *life*. We are given that special place of intercession where we can actually connect with the Holy Spirit and "shake the heavenlies" on behalf of others. We strengthen our relationship with Jesus as we learn to recognize His voice.

Many of us who are in full time ministry are actually terrible when it comes to spending time with the Lord like this. I know pastors who mistake their times of sermon preparation for their own time in communion with Jesus. I know others who mistakenly spend all of their time with Jesus only in intercession for their ministry. The needs press on us from every side, and there doesn't seem to be time for it all. I've struggled with this myself. If the time isn't held as sacred, it's the first thing to go when the day gets hectic.

Something changed when I started receiving revelation about God's affections for me. When I started to realize just how much He loves me— just how much His heart beats with joy when He gazes at me— it all of a sudden became easier to spend time with Him. We have a love relationship with God! Until we really know this, we will continue to struggle in the secret place. It is possible, though, to have this kind of Sabbath rest on a day-to-day basis. Please don't hear me saying that our times with the Lord are dependent upon our feelings, though. There have been many days when I have felt nothing at all in the secret place. Then a morning comes along when He truly meets me, and I come undone. The days of waiting all seem to fade away. *He is absolutely worth it!* Without this kind of relationship, there is no hope for thriving in ministry.

Seasonal Sabbath

THE FIRST KIND OF SABBATH REST God calls us to enter into is the daily secret place. Over the years though, I have begun to recognize that there is another place of Sabbath. This is the kind of Sabbath rest I am engaged with right now. For those of us in ministry, we need to be careful to steal away throughout the year and get away from the daily grind. We need an exit every now and then to get rest, gain perspective, and hear from the Lord. We honestly need at least one day a week where we have no agenda, no plan, and no demands that are able to pull on us. Many people involved in ministry (including me) just don't guard or protect their time this way.

Determine from the beginning of your ministry to have some sacred time set aside each week for you to get rest— for yourself, for your marriage, and for your family. Guard this time jealously! For singles especially, there is a real temptation for you (and others) to look at your time as fluid. Not having a family to think about, when something comes up you think to yourself: "Well, I don't have any commitments, so I can do it." Guard your time jealously!

When I talk about the idea of a weekly Sabbath rest, I don't necessarily mean you have to spend the day *only* in quiet meditation and prayer and Bible Study. Go out, have a good meal with friends, watch a good movie, take a long nap, read a good book, go on a hike, go shopping, or go on a mini-adventure! As a new Christian, I somehow got the idea that true "Holy rest" meant doing something "spiritual." A lot of other college students around me had the same idea. I thank God for Tom, who told us, "Sometimes the most spiritual thing I can do is take a nap or watch TV." A lot of the students who heard it thought it was sacrilegious. It can offend the religious spirit within us to think such things, but I am convinced Tom's words are true. We weren't made for the Sabbath: the Sabbath was made for us! (Mark 2:27)

Take weekly time to rest. For those of you heading into a life of ministry in a cross-cultural setting, I promise you that you are going to need that rest. Especially in the early days of your adaptation, simply navigating culture can be exhausting. Don't underestimate the physical, emotional, and spiritual toll that living in a harsher environment takes on you. In order to keep my visa, I have to leave the country every six months. God knew I was really bad at taking breaks, so He has used the rules to ensure I get that break. Although I was frustrated with these interruptions initially, now I look forward to them because I need them. I take a week in a nearby country, eat western food, and see a couple of good movies. I take long walks, take long naps, enjoy AC, read a couple of good books, and drink lots of coffee. I look at it as a forced vacation.

We must guard not only our daily time and weekly time, but also our seasons of Sabbath. I spent twelve years in Asia without one serious season of Sabbath! That is craziness. I went "home" every year initially for three to four weeks. Then I started going home every 18 months for two to three weeks. Until I arrived for this sabbatical, it had been two and a half years since I had taken any kind of real break. What was I thinking? What military would send a soldier to the front lines of the battlefield with this kind of demand? It's unrealistic, but it's my own fault. It took my nearly dying to believe the message that I needed a Sabbath rest. You must be sensitive to your own emotional and physical needs, as well as the needs of your family. I truly believe that this six month sabbatical (and the ones to come) will enable me to last the long haul in Asia.

The Rhythm of Sabbath

FINALLY, I WOULD LIKE TO DISCUSS a third kind of Sabbath rest. I call it "the rhythm" of rest, and the best way to explain it is by sharing the things that happened to make me realize I *didn't* have it. My life with Jesus has been marked by reading books and writing: books have seriously discipled me! If you asked me anytime over my first ten years in Asia to suggest a good book or to share some deep truth I had learned through a book, I would be eager to do so. I also wrote often in my journal: thoughts, insights, prayers, and Scripture. About a year ago, I picked up my journal and dusted it off and was totally shocked to realize that I hadn't written much in it for months. At the same time, a friend, knowing my affinity for good books, asked me what I was reading.

At any other time, I would have named three different books. I stuttered, though, and realized that I had almost completely lost the habit of reading. When did this happen? Was I really *that* busy? Although I was spending time in the secret place with Jesus, and although I had taken times of short vacations, I had almost lost this practice entirely. The thing is, reading and writing were a part of me. It was one of the things that brought me both deep rest and deep joy. Somewhere along the line, that part of me had withered and almost died. I had lost my rhythm. I don't mean to sound melodramatic, but it's true. Simultaneously, I had begun to lose that deep joy of a life hidden with Christ.

When I talk about this third kind of rest, this "rhythm of rest," I am referring to a lifestyle and deep inner peace that resides in our hearts and spirits. I'm talking about the kind of rest that carries joy deep within and the peace that is completely untouched by circumstances. Beloved, it is possible! We've got to fight for it, though, to guard it jealously, and to let it become a part of who we are. God is restoring it to me even now; He is bringing me back to this simple place of deep rest.

It's one thing to find rest during furloughs, vacations, and sabbaticals. It's quite another to walk in deep rest in the middle of day-to-day life in a harsh environment. It is possible, though, and I want it! There must have been a thousand sermons preached from Matthew 11: 28-30:

> *"Come to me, all you who are weary and burdened,*
> *and I will give you rest. Take my yoke upon you and*
> *learn from me, for I am gentle and humble in heart,*
> *and you will find rest for your souls. For my yoke is easy*
> *and my burden is light."*

These messages talk about how we are supposed to give our burdens to Jesus, to trust Him more, and to walk in rest in hard times (all true). However, I believe that God wants us to live a *lifestyle* of rest. In this place of rest, grounded in deep roots in Him, we don't even have to consciously release our burdens nor take up his yoke. It would already be on us: it would be a part of who we are!

I am convinced that this kind of rhythm of rest is possible. It's hard to define, but easier to describe. It's a place with God where nothing shakes us. Calamity, betrayal, hardship, suffering, misunderstandings, demands, and persecution— nothing shakes us. It's a rhythm in which we can just as easily read a book, heal the sick, take a nap, feed the poor, play with our kids, or preach a sermon. It's a place with the Lord where we walk so intimately with Him that we know His heart, His will, and His voice in everyday life. It's the place where our very day-to-day activities are covered in grace. It's where we are deeply aware of the presence of God, no matter what our circumstances or feelings might be. This rhythm of rest is possible, and it's crucial if we are going to survive in ministry.

As you head towards cross-cultural ministry, do whatever it takes to rest deeply and to rest well. Guard your heart and your time. Determine to set time apart each day to seek God tenaciously. Make sure you schedule weekly and seasonal times of true rest. Ask God to show you how to walk in rhythms of rest with Him. It is possible, and it's easier than we think. Now, excuse me, but I'm going to drink a hot white mocha with whip, eat a blueberry muffin, read a book, pray a bit, and then take a nap. Grace!

Chapter 10

Concluding Thoughts

⌦

IT IS MY DEEP DESIRE to see global workers engaged in ministry across the nations, being totally equipped to not only survive the rigors of life cross-culturally but to actually thrive in such a life! God wants many of you to come, to serve, and to give your life away— but He wants you to do so with open eyes. Too many have romanticized the notion of serving cross-culturally to the point that they head out with completely unrealistic expectations; they are often totally unprepared for what awaits them as a result. I am whole-heartedly committed to the heart of Christ throughout the world, and I long for more workers to come. At the same time, I've seen a lot of brokenness among those who do come. It is my prayer that this small book be an encouragement to many.

I wrote the bulk of this book during my six month sabbatical and finished the final touches upon my return to Asia. As I've shared about this project with friends involved in similar kinds of ministry, they have all commented on how hungry they are to know the secrets of lasting the long haul with joy. I'm hungry myself. I write this handbook as way of encouraging those friends, while at the same time encouraging myself.

Sometimes I hear cross-cultural workers quote Matthew 10:29-31:

> "'Truly I tell you,' Jesus replied, 'no one who has left home or brothers or sisters or mother or father or children or fields for me and the gospel will fail to receive a hundred times as much in this present age: homes, brothers, sisters, mothers, children and fields—along with persecutions— and in the age to come eternal life. But many who are first will be last, and the last first.'"

They use this verse to describe their sacrifice, equating the passage— and their lives— with loss. I can't tell you how many missionaries I've encountered who seem to have resigned themselves to a miserable life in ministry. Remember, though, that I started this little book with the passage from Psalm 16: *"You have made known to me the path of life. You will fill me with joy in Your presence, with eternal pleasures at Your right hand."* This is the truth missing from the hearts of many of my sisters and brothers. Jesus said that He came so that we may have life, and have it to the full. Just because you are serving across the world in hard places doesn't mean you are exempt from this promise. It's for you! It's for me! It's for us.

Even as I write, I recognize that many have given their entire lives away for the sake of the gospel in harder places than where I am. I am fully aware of the kinds of saints mentioned in Hebrews 11— nameless, faceless, cross-cultural workers who have walked before us and of whom the world is not worthy. I tremble before their examples, realizing that I have so much to learn myself. I still feel so new at this, even after almost thirteen years! Yet I write this now as a sister trying to encourage others as they set out to embrace God's heart among the nations.

I wish I had access to a handbook like this when starting out. It certainly could have saved me from a lot of wrong thinking and from making many mistakes. You must weigh what's written here, though: I admit it's rather limited. Compare it to your own experiences and to your own revelations, and always to the Word of God. I pray that you can embrace the parts of the book that speak to your heart and mind.

May God bless you tremendously with joy in *His Holy Spirit* as you seek His heart among the nations. May He fill you with joy in His presence and pleasures at *His right hand*. May you not set the bar too low or settle for too little of God's goodness. May you not just survive in cross-cultural ministry, but may you *thrive*. It is possible to last the long haul with deep abiding joy!!!

|| *Thriving*

Appendix 1

Short-Term Mission Trips: Time for Change?

"Jesus went through all the towns and villages, teaching in their synagogues, proclaiming the good news of the kingdom and healing every disease and sickness. When he saw the crowds, he had compassion on them, because they were harassed and helpless, like sheep without a shepherd. Then he said to his disciples, 'The harvest is plentiful but the workers are few. Ask the Lord of the harvest, therefore, to send out workers into his harvest field.'" Matthew 9: 35-38

THE IDEA OF SHORT-TERM MISSION TRIPS evolved in the 1950's with Operation Mobilization (George Verger). In the 1960's, along came Youth With a Mission (YWAM) with Loren Cunningham. By the late 1970's and 1980's, youth groups and churches started organizing mission trips both to areas close to home as well as those far away. By the 1990's, mission trips had become common in many churches, as well.

Today, it is not uncommon to find people who have gone on not just one short-term mission trip, but two, three, four or five. We have teams visit us in Asia with members who count our trip as their sixth or seventh mission trip! The number of trips and the number of participants on short-term mission trips continues to soar, and they continue to evolve. These trips are often a booming business for ministries and sending agencies, drawing in revenue for some and providing PR for others. At the same time, most of us in long-term cross-cultural ministry are now here because of these short-term trips. Unhealthy patterns that can arise from short-term ministry mentality have strong implications; then again, so do the positive outcomes. So how do we find a balance between this tension?

As a new Christian in college, I had the opportunity to go on my first mission trip. This concept was totally new to me, but I knew it was for me! So a group of us went to Guatemala to help "change the world." We were young, excited, passionate, and on top of the world. What we lacked in wisdom and experience, we certainly made up for in pure zealousness!

We walked the streets of Guatemala City buying juice and food for children who were begging. We painted a rural school. We put on a puppet show in Spanish in a rural village and served lunch one day to a hungry crowd. We took lots of pictures, prayed a lot, sang songs about God's love, and returned home with stories to tell. Looking back on it now, I feel a bit foolish. I also recognize, though, that this was my first step towards a life overseas. In all honesty, the trip was what I call a "scrapbook experience." (Such visits create lots of good stories to tell and photo opportunities. The trip scrapbook then goes on a shelf to be taken down and perused every few years, fondly recalling the memories of the "best mission trip ever!") I confess with shame that I have long since forgotten the names of the children we encountered and befriended. My most vivid memory is that of our day off spent swimming, jumping off waterfalls, and shopping in an outdoor market for souvenirs (and losing my passport on the way to the airport).

The next year a group of us went to Brazil. We wrote letters asking for support, and we prayed for weeks before the trip. We prepared as a team for what was sure to be the most powerful mission trip the world had ever seen! We joined a local pastor there and ministered alongside him in churches day after day, night after night. We visited the favelas and shanty towns. We made friends with the cooks who prepared our breakfasts. We befriended children as we walked back and forth between the "compound" and the "ministry center." We drank Guaraná by the bottle and ate pastries galore! We visited the famous "Christ the Redeemer Statue" and took lots of pictures. God did some amazing things in our team, and in my own heart during this trip. Looking back, I would consider it the second step into my life overseas; unfortunately, it also had hints of another scrapbook experience.

Fast-forward another year, when I was in seminary. An opportunity arose to serve for three months in an orphanage in Jamaica— the chance of lifetime! I was in heaven. I went eagerly, ready to move there permanently if God gave me any leading to do so. It was an amazing experience, and I wouldn't trade it for anything in the world. If I had doubted it before, those three months in Jamaica solidified my destiny. I was made for such a life! The summer gave me the chance to push through the initial phases of cross-cultural ministry and learn to function in a completely different culture. My heart came alive in the process. This was definitely not a scrapbook experience, but rather a clear third step into my eventual lifetime commitment to Asia.

Anyone who has ever been on a mission trip would have to admit that it is life changing. How can you not change when given the chance to see the world through someone else's eyes and to experience another culture? How can it not alter your mindset to encounter poverty and needs to which the Western world is mostly oblivious and to serve alongside the poor? It is always life changing to get a glimpse of a side of God's heart that is virtually impossible to do from the middle-class west. I've often jokingly said that I think God should make it mandatory for all Christians to go on a cross-cultural trip. The relationships we build as we serve ministries are invaluable, and the encounters with God are crucial.

However, there is an ongoing debate among many in the missions community about whether short-term trips are destructive or healthy. Are these teams helpful or harmful? Should they continue to be sent out or not? I learned sometime in middle school that when faced with a big decision, I should list out the pros and cons and then make an informed choice. So with that in mind, I've picked up the following points from friends' blogs, my own experiences, and many conversations with long-term cross-cultural workers.

SOME OF THE PROS of traditional short-term mission trips:

• People who go on such trips gain a better understanding of cross-cultural ministry and God's heart.

• Many are awakened to the financial needs of world mission and become supporters of long-term cross-cultural ministry.

• Short-term trips create a unique discipleship environment for those involved, increase passion for Christ, and increase awareness of and obedience to the Great Commission.

• Short-term trips give way to long-term commitments. I haven't met one cross-cultural worker yet who did not first go on a short-term trip. These short-term trips often help potential long-termers define their calling and gifting.

• When done well, short-term trips provide encouragement to long-term workers. This comes in the form of care packages, supplies, gifts from home, and worship/prayer/conversation in their mother tongue. Teams can be a breath of fresh air for a weary worker: I know they have been crucial for me at points in my own ministry.

• Short-term teams of professionals (i.e. medical workers) can often enhance long-term ministry efforts, as well as opening doors to other areas that long-term workers cannot get into.

• If done well, teams may help to revitalize weary churches and reignite the passion of their workers.

SOME CONS of traditional short-term mission trips:

• They are very expensive. An average trip to a second world context for one week is 1,200 dollars. To go further overseas, it can be as high as 3,000 dollars.

• Aside from airline expense, short-term trips are often financially inefficient. A team of ten Americans can build a church in Mozambique for the price of $28,000. A long-term worker can gather a team of local workers from Mozambique to build the same church for $2,800.

• Teams can take a toll on long-term cross-cultural workers: hosting them is often demanding and exhausting.

• Traditional trips may not have a "kingdom impact" on the recipients. They don't often leave a long-term legacy.

• Some short-termers, by virtue of not understanding the culture, actually do more harm than good in terms of "witness" cross-culturally.

• Trips can contribute to an unrealistic and romanticized view of long-term cross-cultural ministry. Even worse, those who go repeatedly on only short-term trips may actually have their hearts deadened to the radical call of God for sacrificial living. "Mission trip junkies," I call them— people who have visited ten countries in ten years— can't imagine having to plow through culture shock, learn a language, or suffer in any way. They don't know how to persevere under difficulty: two-week trips do not require this kind of sacrifice of them. Their hearts are in the right place, but their overexposure to short-term trips often renders them unrealistic and ineffective.

• Some short-term trips can lean dangerously towards "orphan tourism." They may include time spent at local orphanages among children who have been through too much already. Photos are taken, promises are made, and friendships are forged, only to be forgotten in the months upon returning home. Ministering to "orphans" seems to capture every believer's heart, no matter where they are from, but the damage left behind is unhealthy and destructive.

So, weighing the pros and cons above as I was taught in school, we can safely conclude that short-term mission trips should hereafter be abolished— right? The number of negatives seems to outweigh the positives, so the answer must be to just cancel the short-term trips— isn't it?

Of course not. We all recognize that this suggestion is ridiculous, and the solution is not so simple. What is the remedy, then? The truth is that I don't know if I have a clear answer. I have ideas, though, which may be helpful. Let me try to describe what I believe a whole new model of short-term mission trips might look like.

1) Change the name of the trips.

EVEN THE NAME "short-term mission" gives members the idea that they have a lot to offer, and are, by nature, going to accomplish some great "mission" in the host country. This has strong implications that the "go-er" is somehow the one in power, who has everything to give and to offer. It sets us up to somehow become the "great hope for the nations." I prefer the title "Discovery Trips," "Vision Trips," or "Encouragement Trips." These titles present a more realistic view of what actually happens on such journeys. We head to "X-country" in order to discover more of the world and God's heart for it, and we go as learners and discoverers. We also focus on our desire to encourage the long-term workers. (I've had visitors come whose sole purpose was to bless me and encourage me, and no words can describe how valuable their "encouragement trip" was!) These new titles can help us to be more intentional about our purpose for going.

I think it will be hard at first to start using these kinds of names for most churches, but even a simple step like this can help re-wire our thought processes in terms of short term ministry. We need to be free to call the trip a discovery trip and define the purpose clearly. "We are going to encounter God's heart as we interact in this culture." Discovery teams really are more for the people coming than the missionaries or culture so that the participants can be changed and go back and change their own homes, churches, and culture. It's nothing to feel guilty or ashamed of. Own the purpose. Own it. It does sound better and more spiritual to say, "we are going to change the world," than "we are going to encounter God and change ourselves." However, as MOST know who have actually served cross-culturally, it is those who go who are truly transformed.

It would also be healthy for us to re-evaluate what makes a successful trip. Let's pull away from the traditional gauges of how to measure the success of a cross-cultural trip: how many people got saved? How many heard the gospel? How many people got fed and/ or clothed? How many children attended VBS? How many times did you speak in front of the crowd? How many miracles did you see? How many Bibles did you pass out? Let's move away from the concept of mission trips and towards the concept of discovery trips, simultaneously re-evaluating what our ultimate purposes are.

2) *Spend more time and resources on adequate pre-trip training.*

LEARN ABOUT THE MINISTRY and the culture. For any team visiting Joy Homes, they are required to pay for/ host a friend of our ministry, a "liaison," to come and spend some time with the team in pre-trip orientation. This is ideal, but it may not always be available. Find other resources to help: they are abundant! Spend time going through a simple book that teaches you about the culture (*Culture Shock: X Country, a Survival Guide to Customs and Etiquette*, published by Marshall Cavendish Corporation, is an excellent series). Spend a lot— the majority— of your team time in prayer and worship. This is what is most needed. Make sure that they realize that God wants to do a work in their hearts (not just those of the locals) that will last for eternity. Lastly, train the teams in such a way that they get out of the "tourism" mindset. Teach them to serve, not from the position of a "wealthy educated Christian foreigner" but rather of a humble brother/sister and learner. (Only allowing one camera per team is a practical way we at Joy Homes have started fighting the "tourism" urge.)

---

3) *Stop inventing projects for the teams to do to feel "useful."*

THINK ABOUT IT. Does that church really need to be painted again? Really? I know of some Guatemalan churches that host six or seven vacation Bible schools each summer, so that their summer mission teams will feel useful.

Focus on prayer and worship as the model for "discovery teams." The team may not be able to build a shack for a poor family in Jamaica, but they will be able to help build the Kingdom of God through true prayer and worship. When teams visit us, we tell them up front that they are expected to pray/worship several hours each day. We actually make it mandatory that they bring a worship leader with them! (Unfortunately, this very concept will weed out half of the short-term teams.) We have a book filled with pictures and prayer requests for every child in our ministry, as well as page after page of information about our region and the spiritual breakthroughs needed there. We've actually seen monumental breakthroughs occur in our ministry and in the area after a season of a prayer/worship by a short-term team!

4) *Spend more time in activities related to mercy and social justice.*

A WEEK SERVING IN A LEPROSY HOSPITAL is much better suited to a discovery trip than a week spent performing puppet shows or passing out tracts. What better way is there to encounter God and His heart than to interact and give yourself selflessly among the oppressed and hurting? (By the way, a two-hour trip to visit one of Mother Theresa's homes and a week of serving for six hours per day will produce totally different results. I'm not talking about simply visiting places of ministry, but actually serving there.) When teams come to visit us, we always spend a significant time of mercy ministry in local care centers. They are usually stunned and broken on the first day of serving in such places. By the second day, they have begun to ask questions. By days three and four and five, their hearts have processed some incredibly deep and profound truths about the Kingdom of God. I have asked more than a hundred short-term visitors this question: which part of the trip was the hardest and which part was the best? Their answers are almost always the same— that of their time engaged in acts of mercy in these hard places.

---

5) Stop allowing untrained, unseasoned, unanointed Christians to come in to "teach and equip" local believers.

Do your homework. Investigate thoroughly. Oftentimes, these teaching sessions are established to make the visitor feel useful and needed. Take it from someone on this side of the world— you would be shocked to hear what actually goes on in some of these teaching conferences. Many times, local ministries force all of their workers, as well as the recipients of ministry benefits, to attend the conferences. One of the young people I work with, an eighteen year old single boy, was forced to attend a "pastors weekend conference on family and marriage" along with the other (all young and single) students of his school. The Asian pastor had simply wanted to impress the foreigners (mission team) with the large number of conference attendees. Since the teachers were all young married couples who had never left their home country before, their examples and stories were strange, and even sometimes offensive, to the Asian ear.

6) Team leaders: Research your destination and ministry carefully and learn about giving.

FIND OUT THE DETAILS of what you will be doing and why you are doing it. What are the objectives? What are the actual costs? Learn about the financial situation of the ministry and the local area. Don't lead teams blindly.

Teach your teams about giving. I'm a big advocate of giving, radically and sacrificially, but we must also give wisely. Westerners, especially, are masters at throwing money away. Many come on a trip, handing out money and gifts like candy, and cause unhealthy dependence and manipulation to develop in the hearts of local believers as a result. This solidifies a destructive benefactor-recipient mentality. I have heard visitors jokingly say that they don't mind giving money away in developing nations because it's like "monopoly money" to them (relative to their own culture). The truth is, that's insulting to your host culture. People work hard and long for their money: to have a visitor laugh, overpay, and over-give is condescending. Give money if God leads, but pray first. Ask God to show you how much to give, to whom to give it, and how to give it!

Once, I had a few members of a short-term team stay over an extra week to explore Asia. This husband-wife couple had heard of a poor orphanage about four or five hours from us, and they went to serve there for a week— with beautiful hearts and intentions. On the last day, the pastor and director of the orphanage (which housed 45 girls) cried. He "confessed" to them that the orphanage was completely out of money. They were told that the 30 oldest girls were being taken out of school that very week to work since there was no money. The well-meaning couple cried and prayed along with the pastor, emptied their bank accounts via an ATM, and gave sacrificially to the orphanage. Who could blame them, right? Who would feel right to go back to America with so much while thirty young girls were denied an education?

A mere few months later, another team came to visit. Three of the team members had somehow heard about an "orphanage in need" a few hours away, and they wanted to go visit. It turned out to be the same place, and what do you know? The pastor gave these three American girls the exact same sob story-only made worse. This time the girls were not only going to have to work, but work in the sex-industry if money didn't come in that very day for their education. The American girls emptied their bank accounts then came back through our city, testifying about how God used them and sent them there just in the "nick of time!" I wonder how many westerners this well-spoken and impressive orphanage director had duped along the way, all in the name of Christ? I am begging short-term teams to use discernment!

---

7) Advocate missional living.

GIVEN THE FACT THAT MANY short-termers don't end up moving across continents, we need to be super intentional about Kingdom discipleship. Short-term trip leaders should be experienced and gifted enough to help individuals translate the things they have learned cross-culturally into daily life back at home. We need leaders to help short-term workers make that jump from life during their two weeks in another country to life back at HOME. They should help them wrestle with difficult social justice issues, and they should help guide them in figuring out how to live missionally in their own spheres of influence. Short-term trips can be truly effective if they produce more well-discipled believers who will help to transform their own home culture.

Make sure to spend adequate time, prayer, training, and resources on helping short term discovery teams process their time in cross-cultural ministry: the trip is not likely to have long term impact on the participants if this authentic processing does not take place. Short-termers are usually spiritually hungry and wide open to be challenged after returning from a trip. Take advantage of that! True discipleship at all stages— before, during, and after the trip— is the key to equipping believers to live radically for Jesus when they return home. Done well, short-term trips are potentially one of the most significant methods of intense discipleship available to a leader today. They can inspire a whole generation of Christians to live radically and missionally right where they are.

---

8) Re-evaluate where short-term discovery teams go.

IF EVERY LONG-TERM CROSS-CULTURAL WORKER first comes on a short-term team, then doesn't it make sense to send more teams to completely unreached places? Most teams (because of time and funds) choose destinations close to home (Latin America and the Caribbean for example). However, very few teams choose destinations that actually need long-term workers. We don't see many teams headed to Pakistan, North Africa, or Indonesia. Honduras and Guatemala might be great first step discovery trips for high school and college students and families, but why are they often the sole destinations of many churches too? I challenge you to get away from the safe status quo and begin seeking God about new destinations. Think outside the box a little!

I know a church in the US that is committed to a certain region of the world in the 10/40 window. While they do give some finances to other areas around the globe, they radically give themselves to this particular region. Every long-term worker who wants to go there is trained and supported. Every single short-term trip from the church is to this region, and each team goes to pray, worship, learn to relate, study, and encourage long term workers. As a result, the number of long-term workers from this church in this very difficult part of the world has increased tremendously over the years. This is effective short-term ministry! It's working! Beautiful testimonies are coming out of this area.

People sometimes criticize short-term mission trips with dismissive statements like: "Ugh, they are a necessary evil." I wholeheartedly disagree. The harvest is still plentiful, and the workers are still few. Jesus' words are still true today. Countless lives have been changed during short-term cross-cultural experiences (including mine), and short-term experiences are crucial steps in the long term call to be harvesters. We don't need to throw out the concept of short-term ministry entirely.

What we do need to do is to intentionally address the negative issues surrounding short-term experiences, ensuring that their eternal benefits exceed their detriments. The truth is that short-term trips can be great tools in the work of completing the Great Commission. Let's get together to re-evaluate how short-term missions are done, and let's be willing to think outside the box a little. Let's go, but lets' temper our journeys with wisdom. The harvest is still plentiful, the workers are still few.

Appendix 2

Suggested Reading for Hungry Hearts

Finances

ALCORN, RANDY. *Money, Possessions, and Eternity.* Carol Stream, IL: Tyndale House Publishers, Inc., 2003.

BONK, JONATHAN J. *Missions and Money.* Maryknoll, New York: Orbis Books, 2006.

CORBETT, STEVE AND FIKKERT, BRIAN. *When Helping Hurts.* Chicago: Moody Publishers, 2009.

CUNNINGHAM, LOREN. *Daring to Live on the Edge: The Adventure of Faith and Finances.* YWAM Publishers, 1992.

PLATT, DAVID. *Radical.* Colorado Springs: Multnomah Books, 2010.

Mission Biographies/Help

GRIGG, VIV. *Companion to the Poor.* Waynesboro, GA: Authentic Media, 2003.

JONES, E. STANLEY. *Christ of the Indian Road.* Abingdon Press, 1925.

LENIER, SARAH A. *Foreign to Familiar*. McDougal Publishing Company, 2000.

OLSEN, BRUCE. *Bruchcko*. Lake Mary, FL: Charisma House, 2006.

RICHARDSON, DON. *Eternity in their Hearts*. Ventura, CA: Regal Books, 2006.

RICHARDSON, DON. *Peace Child*. Regal Books, 2005.

Emotional Health

ELDREDGE, JOHN. *Waking the Dead*. Thomas Nelson, 2006.

SCARAZZO, PETER. *Emotionally Healthy Spirituality*. Nashville, TN: Thomas Nelson, 2006.

The Deeper Life

BICKLE, MIKE. *Passion for Jesus*. Lake Mary, FL: Charisma House, 2007.

BROTHER YUN. *The Heavenly Man*. London: Monarch Books, 2002.

DEERE, JACK. *Surprised by the Power of the Spirit*. Grand Rapids: Zondervan, 1996.

EDWARDS, GENE. *100 Days in the Secret Place.* Shippensburg, PA: Destiny Image Publishers, 2002.

ELDREDGE, JOHN. *Journey of Desire.* Nelson Books, 2001.

GRUBB, NORMAN. *Rees Howells, Intercessor.* CLC Publications, 1988.

GUYON, JEANNE. *Experiencing the Depths of Jesus Christ.* Sargent, GA: Christian Books Publishing House, 1981.

JOHNSON, BILL. *Strengthen Yourself in the Lord.* Shippensburg, PA: Destiny Image Publishers, 2007.

JOHNSON, BILL. *When Heaven Invades Earth.* Shippensburg, PA: Destiny Image Publishers, 2009.

MUELLER, GEORGE. *The Autobiography of George Mueller.* New Kensington, PA: Whitaker House, 1996.

NOUWEN, HENRI. *In the Name of Jesus.* The Crossroad Publishing Company, 1992.

NOUWEN, HENRI. *The Way of the Heart.* HarperOne, 1991.

SORGE, BOB. *Secrets of the Secret Place.* Grandview, MO: Oasis House, 2001.

SORGE, BOB. *Unrelenting Prayer.* Oasis House, 2004.

TOZER, A. W. *The Pursuit of God.* Tribeca Books, 2011.

Contact the Author

Contact the author for reduced rates on bulk orders, or just for feedback at *carissaalma@gmail.com.*

You can also join the Carissa Alma (Author) page on Facebook to find out more!

https://www.facebook.com/CarissaAlma

CPSIA information can be obtained at www.ICGtesting.com
Printed in the USA
BVOW05s1508070216

435323BV00006BB/95/P